JO IPPOLITO CHRISTENSEN, author of the best-selling, award-winning *The Needlepoint Book: 303 Stitches with Patterns and Projects,* has taught many courses in needlepoint, including Creative Stitchery at the University of Alaska. She is also the author of *Teach Yourself Needlepoint, Bargello Stitchery, Appliqué and Reverse Appliqué, Needlepoint Simplified,* and others.

BOOKS IN THE CREATIVE HANDCRAFTS SERIES:

The Art of Woodcarving, Jack J. Colletti

Clothesmaking, Linda Faiola

*The Craftsman's Survival Manual: Making a Full- or Part-Time Living
    from Your Craft*, George & Nancy Wettlaufer

Creative Embroidery with Your Sewing Machine, Mildred Foss

The Denim Book, Sharon Rosenberg & Joan Wiener Bordow

Designing in Batik and Tie Dye, Nancy Belfer

Designing and Making Mosaics, Virginia Gayheart Timmons

Designing in Stitching and Appliqué, Nancy Belfer

Experimental Stitchery and Other Fiber Techniques. Arline K. Morrison

Inventive Fiber Crafts, Elyse Sommer

Jewelry-Making: An illustrated Guide to Technique,
    Dominic DiPasquale, Jean Delius, & Thomas Eckersley

Needlepoint: The Third Dimension, Jo Ippolito Christensen

The Needlepoint Book: 303 Stitches with Patterns and Projects,
    Jo Ippolito Christensen

New Dimensions in Needlework, Jeanne Schnitzler & Ginny Ross

The Perfect Fit: Easy Pattern Alterations, Jackie Rutan

The Quiltmaker's Handbook: A Guide to Design and Construction,
    Michael James

The Sewing Machine as a Creative Tool, Karen Bakke

Soft Jewelry: Designing, Techniques & Materials, Nancy Howell-Koehler

Teach Yourself Needlepoint, Jo Ippolito Christensen

Tailoring the Easy Way, Lucille Milani

Weaving, Spinning, and Dyeing: A Beginner's Manual, Virginia G. Hower

Weaving without a Loom, Sarita S. Rainey

THE CREATIVE HANDCRAFTS SERIES

Needl

drawings by: Lynn Lucas Jones

photographs by: Carolyn McVadon & James T. Long

THE THIRD DIMENSION

Jo Ippolito Christensen

A SPECTRUM BOOK

PRENTICE-HALL, INC., Englewood Cliffs, New Jersey 07632

Library of Congress Cataloging in Publication Data

CHRISTENSEN, JO IPPOLITO.
   Needlepoint.

   (The Creative handcrafts series) (A Spectrum Book)
   Includes index.
   1. Canvas embroidery. I. Title.
TT778.C3C484   746.4'4   79-1311
ISBN 0-13-611004-5
ISBN 0-13-610998-5 pbk.

Editorial/production supervision by Carol Smith
Interior design by Dawn L. Stanley
Page layout by Jenny Markus
Manufacturing buyer: Cathie Lenard

Needlepoint: The Third Dimension
by Jo Ippolito Christensen

A SPECTRUM BOOK

Printed in the United States of America

10 9 8 7 6 5 4 3 2 1

PRENTICE-HALL INTERNATIONAL, INC., *London*
PRENTICE-HALL OF AUSTRALIA PTY., LIMITED, *Sydney*
PRENTICE-HALL OF CANADA, LTD., *Toronto*
PRENTICE-HALL OF INDIA PRIVATE, LIMITED, *New Delhi*
PRENTICE-HALL OF JAPAN, INC., *Tokyo*
PRENTICE-HALL OF SOUTHEAST ASIA PTE., LTD., *Singapore*
WHITEHALL BOOKS, LIMITED, *Wellington, New Zealand*

for Popsy

Sampler

Hands that pushed the needle in and out,
eyes that frustration wept off to sleep,
teeth that snapped threads or clenched her small pout,
have long been bones in a dry heap

And yet, she spoke aloud to me today.
Above the flea-market clatter, from the dead,
came clearly her childish voice to say,
in the pattern of faded and rotting thread—

This is my sampler, worked so fine.
I'm Anna Snow and I am nine.

Cea Lampp

Contents

Foreword xv
Preface xvii
A Word of Thanks xix

PART

SUPPLIES AND BASIC PROCEDURES

CHAPTER

Supplies   3

Canvas 3; Needles 9; Yarn 11; Other Equipment 13

CHAPTER

Basic procedures 16

Keeping Yarn **16**; Preparing the Canvas **18**; Handling the Yarn **18**; Stitching with Yarn **19**; Stripping the Yarn **19**; Beginning and Ending Yarns **21**; Rolling the Yarn **23**; Continuous Motion versus Stab Method **24**; Direction of Work **26**; Tension **26**; Thickening and Thinning the Yarn **26**; Direction of Stitching **28**; Compensating Stitches **28**; Mixing Diagonal and Vertical Stitches **28**; Correcting Distortion **29**; Ripping and Mending **29**; Cleaning Needlepoint **30**; Instructions for Left-Handers **31**; Enlarging or Reducing a Design **31**; Transferring the Design **32**

PART

THE METHODS OF
THREE-DIMENSIONAL NEEDLEPOINT

CHAPTER

Two-dimensional needlepoint
that seems three-dimensional 39

Stacked Cubes **39**; Ballet Slippers **40**; Three-Dimensional Cube **43**; Triangle **46**

CHAPTER

Raised Stitches   48
Christmas Wreath Ornament **48**; Black-Eyed Susan Purse **49**; Apple Tree Mirror **51**; Jody's Needlepoint Box **53**; Four Seasons Bell Pull **56**; Scissors Case **61**; Farm **63**

CHAPTER

Needlepoint in the round   67
Basket of Flowers **67**; Christmas Mobile **71**; Bird Necklace **73**; Airplane **74**; Golf Cart **77**

CHAPTER

Detached canvas   84
Christmas Wreath **84**; Bulletin Board **88**; Intertwined Rainbows **91**; House **101**

CHAPTER

Appliqué   107
Landscape Table Top **107**; Car **118**; Mother and Child **121**; Apple **127**

CHAPTER

Mixed media   129
Needlepoint Shop **129**; Black Cat **133**; City Park **137**; Northwest Autumn **147**; Waste Knot, Want Knot **151**

PART III

THE STITCHES

CHAPTER 9

Straight stitches   155

Straight Gobelin **157**; Straight Stitch **157**; Split Gobelin **158**; Brick **158**; Giant Brick **159**; Double Brick **159**; Horizontal Brick **160**; Shingle **160**; Hungarian **161**; F-106 **161**; Bargello **162**; Bargello Line Pattern **163**; Bargello Framework Pattern **164**

CHAPTER 10

Diagonal stitches   165

Basketweave **167**; Continental **169**; Half Cross **171**; Petit Point **172**; Slanted Gobelin 2x2 **173**; Split Slanted Gobelin **173**; Interlocking Gobelin **174**; Lazy Kalem **174**; Stem **175**; Byzantine #1 **176**; Byzantine #3 **177**; Oriental **178**

CHAPTER 11

Box stitches   179

Mosaic **181**; Reversed Mosaic **182**; Diagonal Mosaic **182**; Cashmere **183**; Framed Cashmere **184**; Elongated Cashmere **185**; Diagonal Cashmere **186**; Scotch **187**; Giant Scotch **188**; Tied Scotch **189**; Framed Scotch **190**; Reversed Scotch **191**

CHAPTER

Cross stitches 192

Cross Stitch **194**; Rice **195**; 2x2 Cross **195**; Double Stitch **196**; Upright Cross **196**; Slashed Cross **197**; Slanted Cross **197**; Binding Stitch **198**; Plaited Gobelin **200**; Double Straight Cross **201**; Double Leviathan **202**; Tied Windmill **203**; Smyrna Cross **204**

CHAPTER

Tied, eye, and leaf stitches 205

Tied Stitches **205**; Knotted Stitch **207**; Fly **207**; Couching **208**; *Eye Stitches* **208**; Framed Star **210**; Double Star **211**; *Leaf Stitches* **212**; Diamond Ray **212**; Ray **213**; Leaf #1 **214**; Roumanian Leaf **215**; Close Herringbone **215**; Raised Close Herringbone **216**

CHAPTER

Decorative stitches 217

Buttonhole **219**; Buttonhole in Half-Circle **220**; Chain **221**; Spider Webs **221**; Woven Spider Web **223**; Smooth Spider Web **223**; Ridged Spider Web **224**; Wound Cross **224**; French Knot **225**; French Knots on Stalks **226**; Bullion Knot **227**; Starfish **228**; Thorn **228**; Looped Turkey Work **229**; Cut Turkey Work **230**; Lazy Daisy **231**; Needleweaving **231**; Raised Cup Stitch **232**; Raised Rope **233**; Raised Buttonhole **234**; Raised Buttonhole on Raised Band **235**; Shisha **235**

PART

BLOCKING AND FINISHING

CHAPTER

Blocking   239

Blocking Board **239**; Making the Grid **240**; Blocking **241**; Fastening the Canvas **243**; Stains **244**; Hints **244**; Correcting Distortion **244**

CHAPTER

Finishing   247

Framing **247**; Pillows **253**; Jody's Needlepoint Box **257**; Christmas Wreath **259**

Retail mail order sources   261

Index   263

General Index **263**; Stitch Index **265**

Foreword

Sometimes the best things in life come slowly and piece-meal. This has been my experience in my relationship, both personal and professional, with Jo Christensen.

I first met Jo by proxy. My job as traveling needlework consultant in 1973 took me to many parts of the western United States. Since air travel can be numbing to the senses as well as to the body, a piece of needlepoint was always in my carryon luggage for me to while away the hours between cities. On a flight from Denver to Seattle, my seatmate was a delightful gentleman, Captain Stu Denison, returning to duty at Elmendorf AFB, Alaska. He commented on the piece of Bargello upon which I was working, then said, "I have a friend in Anchorage who is writing a needlepoint book."

"Terrific," I thought, "just what we need, another nee-dlepoint book to add to the dozens already available." "How nice," I replied. "I hope she has a publisher." He assured me that she did and that things were progressing smoothly for the book. I enjoyed the remainder of the flight but really gave no thought at all to the needlepoint book he had mentioned.

A few weeks later, one of the customers in the needle-craft shop in Seattle where I was based introduced herself to me as Jo Christensen of Anchorage, Alaska. She reminded me of my earlier conversation with Captain Denison, but because of time schedules, we did not have a chance to become well acquainted. I still wasn't overly enthusiastic about the prospects of "another needlepoint book."

Then *The Needlepoint Book* arrived on the scene in 1976, and I realized that this wasn't just "another needlepoint book." I loved it, used it, dog-eared it, and wore out two copies of it, but I still had not had an opportunity to personally express my delight in it to the author.

In the summer of 1977, in Dallas, as seminar coordinator for the National Needlework Association, I got that opportunity. Jo reintroduced herself to me, and we were instantly on the same wavelength. We had dinner together, sat up and talked until 3 in the morning—both of us with eyelids drooping and tired bodies but not willing to stop—and caught up on each other as old friends who had not seen one another for years. What did it matter that we were *new* old friends?

In the time since that first meeting, I have stayed in her home, bathed her son P. J., shared my bed with her three cats, singly and en masse; met her cabinetmaker, the fabulous Murray Baxter; introduced her to seashells and bought enough in Biloxi to outfit a 10,000-gallon aquarium; shared the beach at Ocean Springs on Mother's Day 1978 with P. J. and Chris, all three of us acquiring massive sunburns; changed from shopping clothes to banquet clothes with her in a rest room in New Orleans; run up astronomical phone bills between Los Gatos, California, and Ocean Springs, Mississippi; played with the microwave oven and ultrasonic jewelry cleaner in her kitchen, and. . . .

All the preceding sharing has nothing to do with needlepoint and books, you say. Not so. Jo is a good friend, a meticulous worker, organized to a fault, willing to give and accept criticism, and a super sharer. If those are not the characteristics of a writer, I've got my money on the wrong horse. Her books speak for themselves. I wanted to share the person with you. I'll miss her for the next two years while she spends her time with her military family in Turkey (phone calls to Turkey being beyond my financial capacity), but just *think* what a wonderful reunion and sharing there will be between these two old friends when she returns!

Barbara Johnston
Needlework author, designer, and teacher
Los Gatos, California

Preface

Needlepoint: The Third Dimension is the report on my preliminary experiments with texture and depth in needlepoint. It is just the *beginning* of a whole new world in stitchery! Techniques that have never before been done with needlepoint are included in this book.

Now you're thinking, "Wow! This really is advanced stuff!" Not altogether true. Admittedly, some of it is. But for the most part, I've included projects that teach you one three-dimensional technique at a time.

Even if you've never done needlepoint before, you can still try this three-dimensional approach. Part I tells you all you need to know about supplies and basic procedures. There are even a few hints for the advanced stitcher, too.

Part II gets to the fun stuff! Chapter 3 deals with two-dimensional needlepoint that appears to be three-dimensional through optical illusion.

Chapter 4 delves into the world of Raised Stitches. Some of you may have already played with these neat, bumpy stitches before. There's a new twist to many of them, so take a peek. The Black-Eyed Susan Purse uses ribbon to do needleweaving! It makes pretty flower petals.

"Needlepoint in the Round" introduces you to a growing part of needlepoint. Most of the projects are made from plastic canvas, but there's also a bird made from silk gauze! Make a two-foot airplane for your flying buff.

Free-flapping canvas that is attached to a background canvas gives us many interesting kinds of things to try. The projects in Chapter 6, "Detached Canvas," experiment with several aspects of this kind of three-dimensional needlepoint. The Christmas Wreath looks *so* elegant, yet a beginner could make it! The Intertwined Rainbows teach you not to be afraid of the canvas. To assemble it, you must cut the canvas right *between* the stitches. No kidding! (It works, too!)

"Appliqué," Chapter 7, gives you a glimpse of how versatile a design you can make when different-sized canvases are applied to one background canvas. None of these projects is particularly difficult to stitch.

In Chapter 8, "Mixed Media," the five projects presented employ several techniques on one canvas to achieve a truly interesting finished product. Northwest Autumn, which looks frightfully difficult, is really cleverly designed so that it can be reproduced by someone whose repertoire of stitches is limited.

Part III contains eighty-four stitches that you will need to work all the projects. The diagrams are *clear*. Photos show you what they look like when they're stitched. Handy charts give you the characteristics of each of these stitches.

Finally, Part IV gives explicit finishing instructions for each of the twenty-nine projects in the book.

My main purpose in writing this book is to introduce you to the three-dimensional world of needlepoint. I want you to see what can be done with needle, thread, canvas, and a little imagination. Maybe you'd like to try your hand at some of the projects presented here. But I hope this book will serve as an inspiration for you to strike out on your own! Don't be afraid of the yarn and canvas. *Have fun!*

A Word of Thanks

These few words of thanks hardly seem sufficient for the many hours that dozens of people have donated to this book—this more than my others, for so much of it was truly experimental.

Lynn Lucas Jones has come through, again, with very clear drawings of stitches, projects, and assembly procedures. Many of her drawings are reprinted from *The Needlepoint Book* and *Teach Yourself Needlepoint,* both by Jo Ippolito Christensen and both published by Prentice-Hall.

Lots of Jim Long's black-and-white photos are also reprinted from *The Needlepoint Book.* Carolyn McVadon took the rest of the super photos—both color and black and white. Your progress through this book will be eased considerably by their very clear photos.

I feel very privileged for Cea Lampp to have written a poem especially for my book. As I thread each needle I think of nine-year-old Anna Snow stitching a sampler, as I so often do.

Many wonderful people experimented with three-dimensional needlepoint in developing the twenty-nine marvelous projects in this book. Some of them got quite a shock when they discovered just how much work goes into designing a piece! The beautiful results of their work are displayed in the color insert and described in the text. Special thanks to these people for graciously allowing me to share their designs:

Jackie Beaty (Ballet Slippers, Bulletin Board), Nyla Christensen (Four Seasons Bell Pull, Scissors Case, Farm), Jody House (Jody's Needlepoint Box), Barbara Johnston (Three-Dimensional Cube, Triangle), Cynthia M. Pendleton (Mother and Child), Carole Key (Airplane), Linda Kilgore (Apple), Mickey McKitrick (House), Pat Means (Northwest Autumn, Waste Knot, Want Knot), Lois Ann Necaise (Needlepoint Shop), Betty Powers (Christmas Mobile), Mary Savage (Christmas Wreath), Diana Smith (Golf Cart), and Wayne Stephens (Stacked Cubes).

Nina West designed and finished the wooden purse for the Black-Eyed Susan Purse. The Apple Tree Mirror was designed by Ed Sibbett, Jr. (from *Stained Glass Pattern Book: 88 Designs for Workable Projects,* Dover Publications, Inc.; 1976). The lettering for Ballet Slippers was stitched from the alphabets designed by Doris Drake (from *Doris Drake's Needlework Designs,* Book I, pages 47 and 60). And the detached canvas technique is reprinted from Chottie Alderson's *Stitchin' with Chottie—A Casebook of Needlepoint Projects & Techniques, Series 2,* © Chottie Alderson, with the kind permission of the author.

My husband, Major John J. Christensen, USAF, did stitch a project for the book, proofread, and did many odd jobs. But—his biggest contribution came in the way of patience. He overlooked three weeks worth of mail stacked on the kitchen counter, soup-and-sandwich suppers, being late to parties because I was giving instructions to my secretary, shirts that needed buttons, tears over a broken fingernail that would delay my photography schedule for two months, and, sometimes, a harried wife.

Harry Childers, Quinn Elliott, Cea Lampp Linton, Bonnie Long, Pat McGowan, and Wayne Stephens proofread my hen-scratching. Picky, picky. . . .

In addition to designing a project, Jackie Beaty started out as my secretary. She did a great job, but unfortunately (fortunately, for her), she moved before the going got rough!

Peggy George stepped in and became my right arm. When the going did get rough, she was twice as dependable as she had been before. Peggy tied up all the loose ends, typed hundreds of letters (or so it seemed), typed the manuscript (whew!), and kept me from losing my mind! (No, she's not available for another job—I've got her!)

I'm grateful to Bill Beaty and Doyle Raymer for designing, in each of their own fields, imaginative wood and silver creations to complement the needlepoint pieces. Thanks, also, to Willis White of the Whistle Stop, Ocean Springs, Mississippi for concocting lovely frames to go around oddly shaped needlepoint pieces.

And to Murray Baxter goes a very special thank you. Murray designed the gorgeous walnut mirror frame, box, table, and base for the City Park. He inspired me in many of my designs and other endeavors. He hefted plaster molds, served as a photographer's assistant, and a boy Friday! A simple thank you is not enough.

My editor Lynne Lumsden is a joy to work with! Even now that Prentice-Hall is through with my book, it's still *my* book. I appreciate their professionalism. And it's Lynne who sees that this professionalism is maintained.

The people who worked so hard on the aesthetic appearance of this book deserve special mention—Jeannette Jacobs, who supervised every aspect; Dawn Stanley, who designed it; Bob Wullen, whose contributions are too many to even begin listing; and Jenny Markus, who did such a beautiful job on the page layout. Their little touches made the difference.

All the details of manufacturing were so ably taken care of by Cathie Lenard. Alice Harvey, who copyedited the manuscript, has my appreciation for taking care of the fine points with stylistic flair and a light touch. Carol Smith, my production editor who got involved with every aspect and kept things running smoothly, made the whole thing easier. I would also like to acknowledge Spartan Typographers, Inc. for their professionalism in meeting a very tight schedule—and doing it beautifully.

And a special thanks to those whose names I don't even know.

Jo Christensen

SUPPLIES AND BASIC PROCEDURES

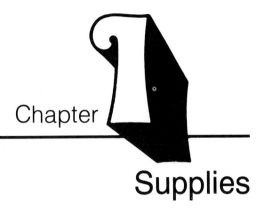

Chapter

Supplies

Needlepoint is fun; it's relaxing. It is an outlet for your imagination and your creative abilities. Three-dimensional needlepoint is new and different from the needlepoint our ancestors did. If you like texture, you will want to try your hand at three-dimensional needlepoint. You do not need to be an experienced stitcher to try it. The projects that are in this book range from the very easy to those that just whet your appetite to do your own.

Because this kind of needlepoint is all from scratch, I'm dispensing with any discussion of all other kinds of needlepoint except that which deals with blank canvas and yarn.

Canvas

Needlepoint is stitched on canvas made especially for it. Threads are woven in a loose grid arrangement, leaving holes through which yarn on a needle is passed. These threads are called mesh.

Buy only the best canvas. You may come to regret it later if you don't. Flaws weaken the canvas, and you cannot make even stitches over them. Any reputable shop owner will gladly cut around flaws for you.

There are basically two kinds of canvas—Penelope and Mono.

Penelope canvas

The canvas threads are woven in pairs. Each *pair* of threads is called one *mesh* (see Figure 1-1). The pair of threads that lies closer together should always run vertically. They are stronger than those that run horizontally. Your eyes may run the mesh all together at first, but eventually it will be easier to see the right hole.

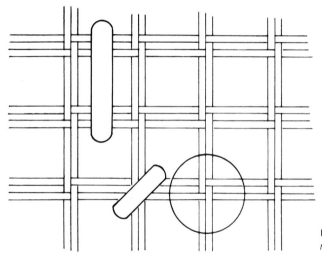

FIG. 1-1 *Penelope canvas (junction of mesh circled).*

Mono canvas

Mono canvas is woven so that one thread equals one mesh. There are two kinds of Mono canvas: Regular and Interlock.

REGULAR MONO CANVAS The threads are woven over, under, over, under, etc. (Figure 1-2). The junction where the horizontal threads and the vertical threads meet is unstable. Only the sizing of the canvas holds them together. As you work on this canvas, the sizing softens, and the mesh move. Working on a frame minimizes this problem.

Stitching Basketweave on Regular Mono canvas also helps to keep it in place. Note that there are special instruc-

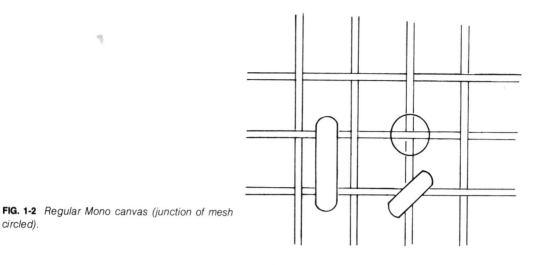

FIG. 1-2 *Regular Mono canvas (junction of mesh circled).*

tions for working Basketweave on Regular Mono canvas (page 168). Many stitches cannot be worked on this canvas. See the section on "How to Read the Diagrams" (page 154) to see how to identify those stitches.

INTERLOCK CANVAS The junctions of mesh are held down on Interlock canvas, sometimes called Leno (Figure 1-3). A separate thread is twisted around the mesh to do this job. This interlocking of the mesh keeps the canvas from raveling easily. This is why we *MUST* use Interlock any time we cut the canvas anywhere other than around a square, rectangular, or round needlepoint piece.

The chart on page 6 gives the pros and cons of Regular Mono and Interlock canvas.

FIG. 1-3 *Interlock Mono canvas.*

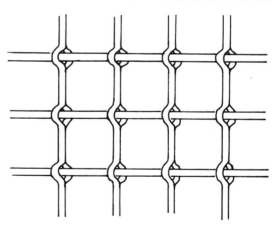

REGULAR MONO CANVAS

Pro	Con
• Round thread, covers better	• Stitch tensions cause it to distort more easily
• Soft, good for pulled thread	• Softness causes distortion more easily
• Basketweave has even more give than on other canvases	• *MUST* stitch on a frame
• Needed for appliqué	• Hard for beginners to learn on

INTERLOCK MONO CANVAS

Pro	Con
• Helps maintain even stitch tension, invaluable for beginners	• Harsh, but softens as you stitch
• Finishing is easier, because it does not ravel easily	• Harshness shreds yarn, must stitch with shorter yarn
	• Cannot use for appliqué

Canvas mesh count and stitch size

After the words *Penelope* and *Mono,* there appears a number. This number tells us how many mesh there are per linear inch. This is not accurate over a large area. If you need 40 mesh on 10 canvas, count out 40 mesh. DO *NOT* measure four inches.

Penelope canvas comes in 3½, 4, 5, 7, and 10. Mono is available in 8, 10, 12, 13, 14, 16, 18, 20, 22, and 24. Penelope 10 is the most versatile canvas. Cross Stitches do best on Penelope 7 or 8. Straight Stitches and Bargello do best on Mono 14. (See Figure 1-4a–h for examples of canvas mesh count.)

FIG. 1-4a *Penelope 4 worked with rug yarn.*

FIG. 1-4b Penelope 7 worked with rug yarn.

FIG. 1-4c Penelope 10 canvas worked with Persian yarn.

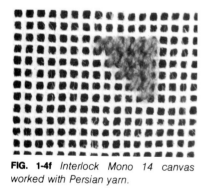

FIG. 1-4d Interlock Mono 10 canvas worked with Persian yarn.

FIG. 1-4e Nylon canvas, 10 mesh per inch.

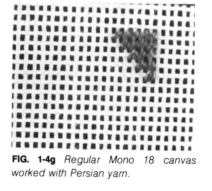

FIG. 1-4f Interlock Mono 14 canvas worked with Persian yarn.

FIG. 1-4g Regular Mono 18 canvas worked with Persian yarn.

FIG. 1-4h Silk gauze 40 worked with embroidery floss.

Needlepoint is divided into three sizes: Petit Point, Gros Point, and Quickpoint. Petit Point is 16 mesh per inch and smaller. Gros Point is 8 to 14 mesh per inch. Quickpoint is worked on rug canvas 3½ to 7 mesh per inch.

Plastic canvas

Plastic canvas is a boon to finishing. It does not ravel. It comes in the three mesh sizes; 5, 7, and 10. It can be bought by the yard, the sheet, in small and large circles, small and large squares, small diamonds, and small hexagons. Some of these are shown in Figures 1-5a–c. Because plastic canvas does not bend easily, it is awkward to work on.

FIG. 1-5a *3" plastic square (7 mesh per inch).*

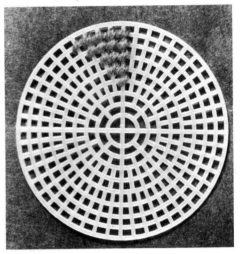

FIG. 1-5b *3"-diameter plastic circle worked with Persian yarn.*

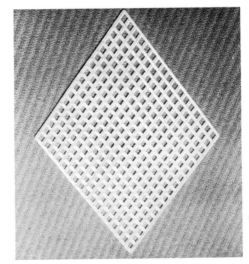

FIG. 1-5c *Plastic diamond.*

Beware of Breakaway (waste) canvas (Figure 1-6). It is made for stitching Cross Stitches onto fabric. When it is wet, the sizing dissolves and the canvas is limp. The mesh are thin and have absolutely no strength at all. *DO NOT use it for needlepoint.*

Needles

A blunt-end tapestry needle is used for needlepoint (Figure 1-7). The needle must pass easily through the hole in the canvas. It should not distort the mesh as it goes through the hole. Yet its eye must be big enough to hold the thickness of yarn needed to cover the canvas. The following chart should serve as a guide in selecting the proper-sized needle.

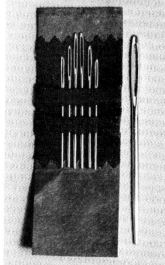

CANVAS SIZE	NEEDLE SIZE
3–5	13
7–8	16
10	18–20
12–14	20
16–20	22
22–24	24

FIG. 1-7 *Blunt-end tapestry needles: Sizes 22, 20, 18, 18, 20, 22, and 13 (from left to right).*

Threading the needle

Some of my students think threading the needle is the hardest part of needlepoint. And let's face it—it's absolutely essential to doing needlepoint!

If you can keep up with a little piece of paper, the method shown in Figure 1-8a & b works every time.

I give the yarn tip an extra twist (making it more tightly twisted) and put it between the end of my left thumbnail and

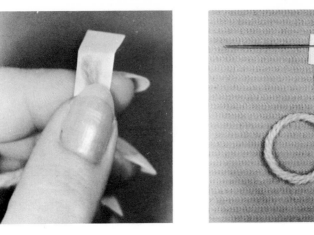

FIG. 1-8 *Threading the needle—the paper method.*

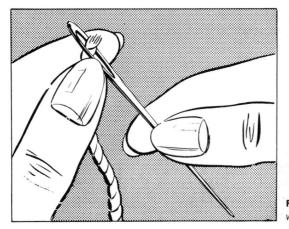

FIG. 1-9 *Threading the needle—my way.*

my index finger. Then I slip the needle between my fingers (Figure 1-9). Most of the time, it works. If it doesn't work, I then fold the yarn over the tip of the needle, squeeze my nail against the needle, and then pass the folded yarn through the eye (Figure 1-10a–c).

A metal needle threader may be your bag. Try it. To keep it always at hand, tie it to your canvas with a piece of yarn.

Sometimes, no matter what, threading the needle turns out to be a failure. If it is, turn the needle over—it seems to me that the eye is bigger on one side of some needles than the other. My engineer husband argues that it is impossible for the hole to be bigger on one side than the other—something about interface or whatever. So—for you needlepointing engineers—the *opening appears* to be bigger on one side than on the other!

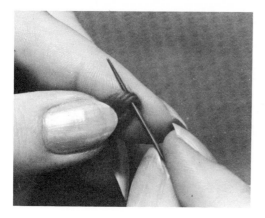

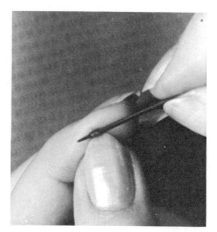

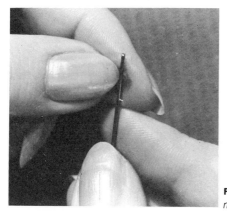

FIG. 1-10a–c *Threading the needle—the loop method.*

Yarn

There are lots of kinds of yarns that can be used for needle-point. However, for the most part, yarns made especially for needlepoint are used. They are made with long, strong fibers that help it to stand up against the harsh canvas. It is also mothproofed.

Needlepoint yarn comes in dye lots. This means the color can vary from one vat of dye to the next. This means you should buy all the yarn you need for your project at one time. If you do need to continue one piece in a new dye lot, work it in by using the method for shaping (page 108).

There are two kinds of needlepoint yarn: tapestry and Persian.

Tapestry yarn

FIG. 1-11a *Four-ply tapestry yarn.*

Tapestry yarn (Figure 1-11a) is a tightly twisted 4-ply yarn that looks like knitting worsted. It is sold in skeins of 100, 40, 12½, 10, or 8.8 yards. The tight twist makes a smooth stitch, but it also makes separating the plies for shading or for thickening and thinning the yarn very difficult. When you do separate tapestry yarn, the stitch no longer looks smooth. For the most part, tapestry yarn does not come in as broad a range of colors as Persian yarn does.

Persian yarn

FIG. 1-11b *Three-ply Persian yarn.*

Persian yarn (Figure 1-11b) is a loosely twisted 3-ply yarn. Each of the 3 plies is a 2-ply strand that is not meant to be separated. So actually Persian yarn is 6 ply. But in this country this fact is overlooked, and each 2-ply portion of the yarn is called 1 ply. This, then, makes the whole a 3-ply strand instead of a 6-ply strand. The 3 plies are readily separated, and shading and thickening and thinning are easily accomplished. Persian yarn comes in lots and lots of *marvelous* colors! There are many colors in one family. These make beautiful Bargello patterns. Persian yarn comes by the strand (about 66"), ounce, and pound as well as by the skein. Quality of Persian yarns varies greatly. Price is usually a good guide.

Novelty yarns

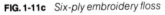

FIG. 1-11c *Six-ply embroidery floss*

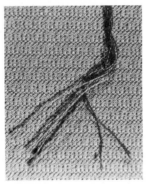

Novelty yarns add texture and interest. They must be used with caution, however, because they are not as strong as needlepoint yarn, and the harsh canvas takes its toll on the novelty yarns. Use a shorter strand (see "Handling the Yarn," page 18) than you would of needlepoint yarn. Also, use novelty yarns only on items that will not receive hard wear, as they do not wear well. Projects in this book use the following novelty yarns: embroidery floss (Figure 1-11c), metallic yarn (Figure 1-11d), velvet or velour yarn (Figure 1-11e; see also "Stitching with Yarn," page 19), pearl cotton (Figure 1-11f), rayon floss (Figure 1-11g), and ribbon (⅛" wide, made especially to stitch with; Figure 1-11h).

SUPPLIES AND BASIC PROCEDURES

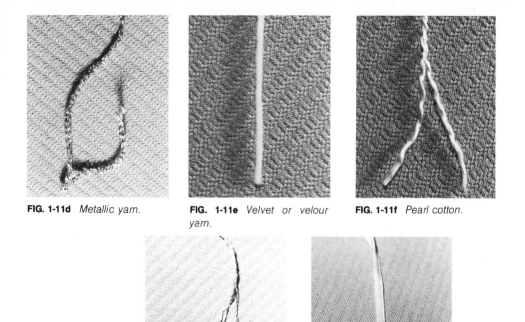

FIG. 1-11d *Metallic yarn.*

FIG. 1-11e *Velvet or velour yarn.*

FIG. 1-11f *Pearl cotton.*

FIG. 1-11g *Four-ply rayon floss.*

FIG. 1-11h *Ribbon.*

How much yarn to buy

To figure out how much yarn you need, you should ideally work 1 square inch of the stitch you want on the canvas you will use with the same color and brand of yarn you will use. Keep track of how much yarn it took. Then calculate the number of square inches in your design. Multiply this figure by the amount of yarn you used. This will tell you how much yarn you need.

Of course, this is not always feasible. A competent shop owner should be able to help you, too. (You can find a complete chart on the amount of yarn needed to work a particular stitch on Mono or Penelope 10, 12, and 14 canvas on pages 9–19 in my book *Teach Yourself Needlepoint,* Prentice-Hall, 1978.)

Other equipment

Needlepoint really doesn't require much else besides canvas, needle, and yarn, but the quality of these other things should be good (Figure 1-12).

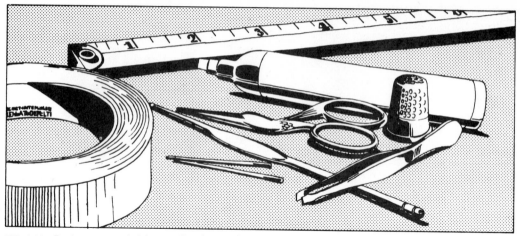

FIG. 1-12 *Equipment needed for needlepoint.*

You will need two pairs of scissors. A pair of fine-pointed, sharp embroidery scissors is needed to cut the yarn and for ripping (sorry to mention it)! A pair of large, crummy scissors is necessary to cut canvas—*nothing* dulls scissors the way canvas does. Tweezers help in ripping (page 29).

Masking tape is needed to bind the raw edges of the canvas. (The cheap stuff doesn't stick very well.) Adhesive tape and freezer tape work well, too.

You will need a ruler to measure canvas. A fine crochet hook is invaluable in burying short tails of yarn. Use a thimble if you are used to one.

Use a *waterproof marker* or *acrylic paint* to draw on your canvas. Do not trust the marker's manufacturers when they tell you that it is waterproof. *Test it yourself* on every *brand* of canvas that you buy. Write on a scrap of canvas. Let it dry thoroughly—overnight is best. Hold the canvas under running water. Blot with a white tissue. If you see color, do not use that marker on that brand of canvas. Save it—it may work on another brand of canvas. Many times a marker is permanent on many surfaces other than those that are highly sized, or starched, as needlepoint canvas is. *Test it yourself.*

FIG. 1-13a *Scroll frame.*

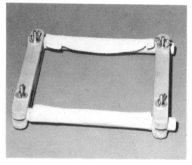

A frame (Figure 1-13a) is essential to even stitches, and a canvas that distorts very little. A scroll, or rotating, frame allows you to roll your work up on opposite sides. Attach your canvas to the twill tape on the roller bars by sewing (Figure 1-13b). Put the edge of the canvas *under* the tape. Arrange the frame so that the wing nuts will be on top. If you put them on the bottom, they snag your clothes as you work.

SUPPLIES AND BASIC PROCEDURES

FIG. 1-13b *Attach canvas to twill tape by sewing.*

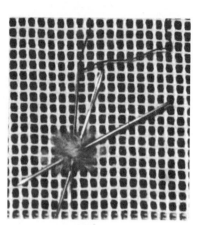

FIG. 1-13c *Stitch a Double Leviathan stitch to park needles.*

Caution must be taken in using a scroll frame in three-dimensional needlepoint. Rolling the canvas will crush any three-dimensional work done.

Chapter

Basic procedures

The following is advice from me to you on how to achieve a professional-looking needlepoint piece. All of the hints are practical; some are general, and some are quite specific.

Somewhere along the line, some people have forgotten that needlepoint is supposed to be fun. Don't become one of them. If rolling the yarn (page 23) bugs you, then don't do it. It's that simple. I'm not saying abandon all hope of creating quality work—I'm saying strive for a level of excellence that you are comfortable with. You may want to vary the degree of quality you strive for with the project you're working on. If you're stitching a family heirloom, by all means, do the best you can; follow all the rules. If you've lost three needlepoint key cases in the last six months and you don't expect number four to last very long, then don't put your all into it.

Try out all the hints, and then decide which approach you want to take. But throughout it all, don't forget—NEEDLEPOINT IS FUN!

Keeping yarn

Use the plastic holder from beer or soda pop to organize the yarn for your current project (Figure 2-1a & b). An embroidery hoop also works. Knot your yarn for storage as shown in

FIG. 2-1a *Yarn for current project looped on plastic holder for soda and beer.*

FIG. 2-1b *Remove one strand for use.*

Figure 2-2a–d. This keeps it free from tangles. To untie, simply pull the ends.

Always keep the color number or the label from your yarn, so you will know what to buy if you want more. Tape a snip of the yarn to the label.

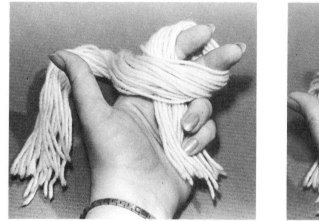

FIG. 2-2a–d *Knotting yarn for storage.*

Basic procedures

17

Preparing the canvas

FIG. 2-3 *Bind canvas with tape.*

Before you start to stitch, there are a few simple steps you need to take. First, measure the canvas carefully. Then cut between the mesh in a straight line. Even if your design is not a square or rectangle, cut the canvas that way. It will make blocking easier.

Bind the raw edges of the canvas with tape—masking, freezer, or adhesive (Figure 2-3). Rub the scissors handle over the tape to make it stick better. Canvas ravels easily after the sizing has been softened with handling. Tape *NOW;* don't wait for it to ravel before you get around to it. Even Interlock Mono, which doesn't ravel readily, needs to be taped to keep the yarn from snagging on the raw edges.

If you don't stitch on a frame, carefully roll the canvas so you can reach the middle (Figure 2-4). *Never crumple the canvas.* Use large safety pins (or diaper pins) to hold the roll in place.

FIG. 2-4 *Roll the canvas for easy access to working area; pin with large safety pins.*

Handling the yarn

Needlepoint canvas is quite rough. Drawing the yarn in and out, hole after hole, wears it thin. If your yarn is too long, the stitches made with the end of the yarn will not be as fat as those made with the beginning of the yarn. So the length of the yarn is critical. On 10, 12, or 14 canvas, a strand 18″ or 20″ is about right. A longer strand of yarn can be used for bigger canvas and for Bargello (even though it is worked on 14 canvas—because the stitches are long). A shorter yarn should be used for smaller canvas. Novelty yarns must be quite short.

When Persian yarn comes by the ounce, the strands are around 66″ long—some shorter, some longer. Cut these strands into thirds for 10, 12, and 14 canvas (except Bargello). Cut them in half for larger canvas and Bargello. For those kinds of Persian and tapestry yarns that come by the

SUPPLIES AND BASIC PROCEDURES

skein, untwist the skein, and cut the 66″-circumference circle once. Then cut that length into thirds. Then knot as shown earlier in Figure 2-2.

When tapestry yarn comes like the skein pictured in Figure 2-5, simply cut the loops at *one* end. Leave the label on. You can then pull one strand from the looped end of the skein.

Some yarns come in skeins that do not lend themselves to any of the foregoing methods. Wrap the yarn around a book or a box that measures 18″ to 20″ in circumference. Cut the circle once, and knot for storage.

FIG. 2-5 *Cutting a skein of yarn.*

Stitching with yarn

Yarn has *nap*. This means that it is smoother one way than the other. If you closely examine yarn that has been cut twenty-four hours or more, you will notice that the yarn has relaxed more at one end than at the other. This end is called the Blooming End (Figure 2-6). It is this Blooming End that is threaded through the eye of the needle. However, before you thread the needle, you need to strip Persian yarn.

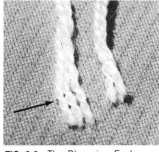

FIG. 2-6 *The Blooming End.*

Stripping the yarn

Stripping the yarn makes Persian yarn plumper. It gets matted together in shipping. A plumper yarn covers the canvas better. Stripping is merely separating the three plies and putting them back together again. I think it's easier to hold the Blooming End between the thumb and index finger of one hand and run two fingers between the three plies (Figure 2-7).

Stripping helps you to double-check to see if the nap of the yarn is right. Sometimes it's hard to tell which end is blooming. If you have the right end, the strand will strip easily. If it does not, turn the strand upside down and try again. It should strip more easily now.

After you've stripped the yarn, run your hand down the strand several times. (Don't let go of the Blooming End yet.) This *stroking* of the yarn will get the extra fuzzies off the strand of yarn. Some yarns are hairier than others. Stroke more or less, according to your judgment.

FIG. 2-7 *Stripping the yarn.*

Basic procedures

When stitching Diagonal Stitches on Mono 14 with Persian yarn, only two plies are needed. You may have noticed that sometimes these two plies cover the canvas and sometimes they don't. This can be corrected if you watch carefully which ply you remove.

Take a *good* look at a strand of Persian yarn. In every strand there is a fat, a medium, and a skinny ply. Now, we've always laid one of the three aside and used the odd one with the odd one from another strand. This way, we get three 2-ply strands from two 3-ply strands. If we always take the medium away when we separate (or thin) the yarn, we will always have yarns of equal thickness (Figure 2-8a & b). So, one fat and one skinny makes the same thickness as two mediums, and each strand will cover as well as the one before it.

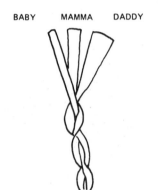

FIG. **2-8a** *Baby, Mamma, and Daddy.*

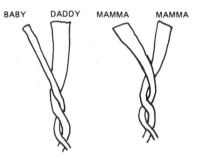

FIG. **2-8b** *One Baby + one Daddy = two Mammas.*

FIG. **2-9** *Move the needle along the yarn as you use it.*

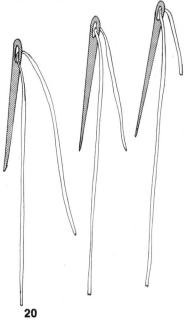

Hint: If you are having trouble telling which is which, put a little tension on the yarn. Sometimes it helps. If you still cannot tell them apart, it won't make that much difference which one you choose. This problem does not arise often.

After you've threaded the needle, fold the yarn almost in half (Figure 2-9). Slide the needle along the yarn as you stitch. This keeps the needle from wearing a thin spot on the yarn. There is only one exception to this rule. When using velour yarn, do just the opposite. Start with the needle about an inch from the end of the yarn. The canvas does not wear the yarn thin, but the needle does wear a thin spot in the yarn. Keep moving the needle in on the yarn (instead of out toward the end). The reason for this is that every bit of yarn past the eye will have to be thrown away, and we don't want to throw away any more than we absolutely have to.

As you stitch with the yarn, keep the same twist you started to stitch with. When the yarn twists too much—or untwists—hold your canvas upside down (Figure 2-10a) and let the yarn and needle dangle and untwist (Figure 2-10b). The stitch you choose causes the needle to turn during

SUPPLIES AND BASIC PROCEDURES

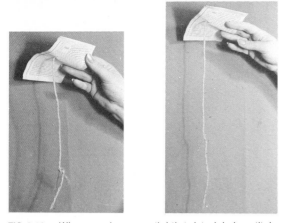

FIG. 2-10a *When yarn becomes tightly twisted during stitching, turn canvas upside down.*
FIG. 2-10b *Let needle dangle until yarn untwists.*

stitching, thus twisting more or untwisting the yarn. As you become more experienced, you will be able to turn your needle enough to correct the twist of the yarn.

Beginning and ending yarns

NEVER knot yarn for needlepoint. To start the first yarn on a blank canvas, pull the needle through from the wrong side of the canvas to the right side, leaving about an inch of yarn for a tail. As you take the first few stitches, be sure to catch the tail. Work over it until it is covered (Figure 2-11).

Use the *waste knot* when working on a frame or when working with a thread so slippery that the above method will not hold the tail. First, knot the yarn (just this once!) (Figure 2-12a–d). Put the needle *down* into the canvas from the right side, leaving the knot on the right side. Bring the needle up to the right side of the canvas about an inch from the knot. Position the re-entry point so that your first stitches cover the tail. When you come to the knot, simply cut it off (Figure 2-13a & b).

FIG. 2-11 *Catch yarn tail on wrong side of canvas with needle, and continue catching tail until completely buried.*

To end the yarn, weave it over and under the back side of the stitches you've just worked. Clip the yarn closely (Figure 2-14a).

Begin subsequent yarns by burying the ends under stitches that have already been worked—on the wrong side, of course. Try to bury yarns in the same color. This makes it easier to rip, should you have to (Heaven forbid!). Never bury a dark yarn under light-colored stitches. It *will* show on the right side.

Basic Procedures **21**

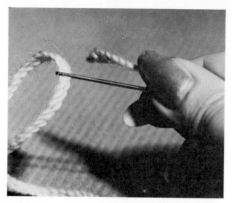

FIG. 2-12a *To make a good easy knot quickly, place end of yarn over eye of needle.*

FIG. 2-12b *Wrap yarn around needle three times.*

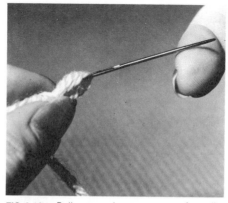

FIG. 2-12c *Pull wrapped yarn over eye of needle and down yarn.*

FIG. 2-12d *And presto! There's a knot!*

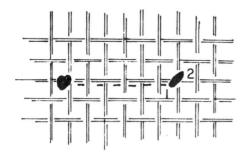

FIG. 2-13a & b *Using the waste knot.*

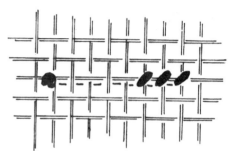

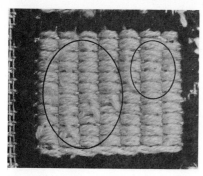

FIG. 2-14a *Clip ends closely after burying tails. This makes a neat back. Long ends look messy, get caught in other stitches, and make lumps on the right side of the canvas.*

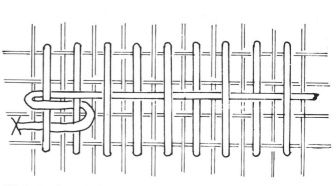

FIG. 2-14b *Bargello Tuck.*

The over–under weaving method to bury the tail is not always secure enough for long, loose stitches and for stitches that have a lot of stress on them (like Spider Webs and the Binding Stitch). Take a Bargello Tuck in these cases (Figure 2-14b). It is simply a Backstitch, taken after you've woven the tail in but before you bring the needle to the right side of the canvas.

If there is no backing to speak of, merely weave the end in and out of a few mesh of the blank canvas. Be sure this area will later be covered by stitches. A good example is the Spider Web (page 221).

Don't stop and start your yarn in a time or pattern. Lumps and lines may show on the right side of the canvas. Don't carry your yarn from one area of stitching to another for more than 1″ or 1½″. When you do, weave it in the backs of the stitches in the area you're skipping.

Rolling the yarn

Sometimes one stitch does not quite cover the canvas, even on the same strand of yarn. This is because the yarn has become overly twisted or does not lie smoothly on the canvas. Rolling the yarn corrects the problem.

Use two hands—one on top of the canvas and one underneath the canvas. Smooth the plies of the yarn as shown in Figures 2-15a–e. Use another needle or your finger to coax the yarn plies into lying on the canvas side by side. You will get a smoother, more professional-looking stitch that covers better.

Basic procedures

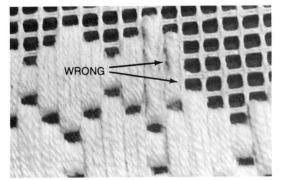

FIG. 2-15a *Wrong stitches need rolling.*

FIG. 2-15b *Rolling yarn with needle.*

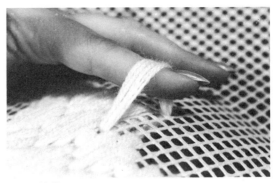

FIG. 2-15c & d *Rolling yarn with fingers.*

FIG. 2-15e *Correct results.*

Continuous motion versus stab method

Continuous motion is like sewing—inserting the needle into the canvas and bringing it out again—all in the same motion (Figure 2-16). You can achieve speed, rhythm, and even

FIG. 2-16 *Continuous motion.*

stitches when you work without a frame. Continuous motion cannot be used with a frame, because the canvas *should* be too taut. If you do use it with a frame, your canvas is not taut enough.

The *stab method* is used with a frame and on plastic canvas. Your dominant hand is constantly below the canvas, and the other hand is on top of the canvas. Both hands work together. When you're using a frame you must hold or working on plastic canvas, use the method in Figure 2-17a & b.

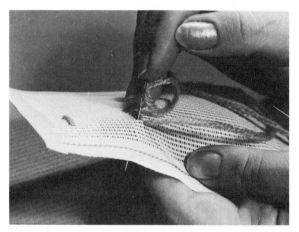

FIG. 2-17a & b *Stab method.*

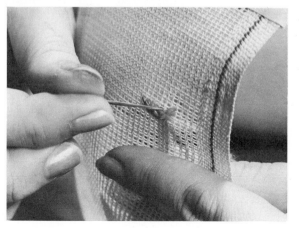

Direction of work

Insert the needle into the canvas so that it goes *down* into a full hole and comes *up* out of an empty hole. This reduces the possibility of splitting the yarn of already worked stitches. However, you don't always have a choice.

Tension

The tension of your stitches should be even. Each stitch should hug the canvas, not choke it. Figure 2-18a–c shows correct tension and stitches that are too loose and too tight. Do not confuse the ripple of the canvas that comes with too-tight tension with the distortion that some stitches cause. In the case of stitch distortion, the canvas will lie relatively flat on a table. Note that long stitches need to be pulled slightly tighter than short ones. (See Mosaic and Scotch Stitches on pages 181 and 187.)

FIG. 2-18a *Correct tension.*

FIG. 2-18b *Too-tight tension.*

FIG. 2-18c *Too-loose tension.*

Thickening and thinning the yarn

Unfortunately, the thickness of yarn varies with its type (tapestry or Persian), brand, and color. So I can't tell you always to use a certain number of ply with a certain stitch and be sure that it will always cover the canvas. The type, size, and brand of canvas also causes the number of ply to vary (Figure 2-19).

Yarn must be thickened or thinned to get a stitch of the proper size. This process is *much* easier with Persian yarn.

To thicken, simply add one or two plies from another strand of yarn to a three-ply strand. This will make a four-ply or five-ply strand. Stripping the yarn will make the thickening invisible. Beware of thickening too much. The stitch pattern can be obliterated, or the canvas can be made to bulge. To thin, simply remove one or two plies.

Play with your stitch, yarn, and canvas in order to find the right combination for your project.

Sometimes adding one ply makes the yarn too thick, or subtracting one causes the canvas to show. This grin-through of canvas can be minimized if the canvas is painted.

Another trick in covering the canvas is to add a French Knot (page 225), a Tramé (Figure 2-20), Frame Stitch (Figure 2-21), or Backstitch (Figure 2-22).

FIG. 2-19 *Stitches on left show yarn so thin that it does not cover canvas; stitches on right were worked with thickened yarn and cover properly.*

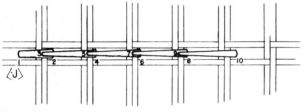

FIG. 2-20 *Tramé.*

FIG. 2-21 *Frame Stitch.*

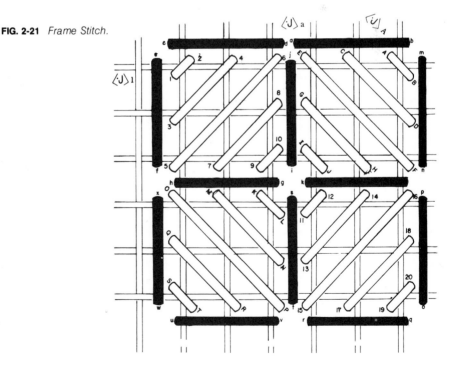

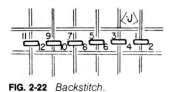

FIG. 2-22 *Backstitch.*

If, when you've finished stitching, you think you should have used one more ply, don't despair. Just stitch right over what you did with one more ply. This won't work for complicated stitches.

Direction of stitching

Work the design of your piece, and then work the background in one direction. The stitch you choose will determine whether you go right to left, top to bottom, etc. If you skip around, your design pattern will not meet.

Compensating stitches

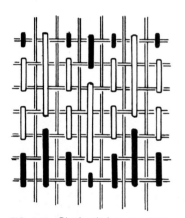

FIG. 2-23 *Black stitches are compensating stitches for the Hungarian Stitch.*

When you use a Decorative Stitch, there's always space between the last whole motif of your stitch and the edge of your area to be covered. This space must be filled with as much of the motif as you can fit into the space. These stitches are called *compensating stitches.*

Establish your pattern across the widest part of your design area. Work as many whole motifs as you can. Then go back and do the compensating stitches (Figure 2-23).

Try to do as much of the stitch as you can. Then stop on your line. If you need help in seeing what the compensating stitches look like, lay a piece of paper over the drawing of the stitch where your design's line cuts the motif. Hold your needlepoint to the light and check for missed stitches.

Mixing diagonal and vertical stitches

Diagonal stitches and vertical stitches do not go well together, but a simple trick helps the situation. Work the diagonal stitches first. Then stitch a row of tent stitches around the diagonal stitches in the same color as the vertical stitches. Then work the vertical stitches, sharing the hole (Figure 2-24).

SUPPLIES AND BASIC PROCEDURES

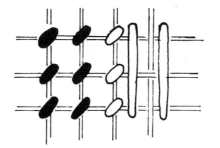

FIG. 2-24 *Mixing diagonal and vertical stitches.*

Correcting distortion

Some stitches distort the canvas. Using a frame keeps this down, but it still happens. Never use stitches that distort (see charts in Part III) on projects that do not have a rigid framework to hold the canvas permanently in place. The Diagonal Stitches and Box Stitches are the worst of the lot.

Ripping and mending

Even the best of us have to rip once in a while. So, blessed is a cheerful ripper! See Figure 2-25a & b for the proper method of ripping.

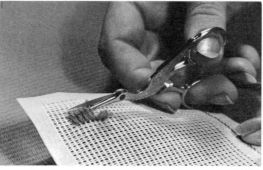

FIG. 2-25a *To rip, cut stitches on right side of canvas. (Be careful not to cut canvas.)*

FIG. 2-25b *With tweezers, pull out incorrect stitches from wrong side of canvas.*

Never reuse yarn that you have carefully ripped. It will be way too fuzzy by the time you pull it through the holes for the third time—in (once), out (twice), and in again (three times).

Once the wrong stitches are out, you will have to rip a few good ones to get enough yarn to work the ends in. A crochet hook makes quick work of this chore.

Do *not* cut the canvas. However, if you do, all is not lost. Cut a patch (Figure 2-26a), and put it under the cut. Stitch as shown in Figure 2-26b. Be sure the patch is on the wrong side of the canvas.

FIG. 2-26a *To mend canvas, cut patch slightly bigger than hole.*

FIG. 2-26b *Work needlepoint stitches through both pieces of canvas as if they were one piece. (Wrong side of mended area shown.)*

Cleaning needlepoint

Needlepoint can be cleaned. But cleaning removes the sizing, and the canvas loses its stiffness and, thus, some strength.

Mild soap and cold water is best for cleaning needlepoint. Rinse well. Roll in terry towels. Block immediately (see page 241).

Premature rotting of wool and canvas and the running of colors has been blamed on Woolite, Scotchguard, commercial needlepoint cleaners, and other similar products. The problem lies in the mixture of chemicals.

Did you ever have a chemistry teacher give a very impressive demonstration with two safe chemicals? When the two harmless chemicals were poured together, there was a volatile reaction.

The paint or marker used to mark the design is a chemical. Yarn is dyed pretty colors with chemicals. Cleaners are chemicals. Scotchguard is a chemical. Add them together with water, and sometimes ugly things happen. So, why take a chance? Omit all the chemicals you can.

Wool needs to breathe. Don't put it next to foam rubber or under glass.

Instructions for left-handers

Left-handed people *can* do needlepoint. Most of the left-handed people I have taught have learned to interpret right-handed instructions into their own jargon.

If you haven't, try turning the drawings upside down. Reverse "right" and "left" and "up" and "down." Hold the canvas any way you like—as long as the result is the same (Figure 2-27a & b).

Use my hints or your own, but enjoy needlepoint, and don't be discouraged because you're left-handed.

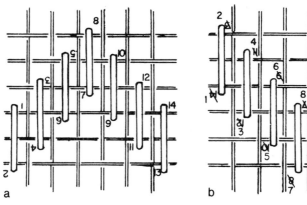

Fig. 2-27a & b *Left-handers, take diagram shown in a and simply turn it upside down as shown in b, following the numbers of the stitches in reverse order.*

Enlarging or reducing a design

Some of the designs in this book will need enlarging. You may have a *lithographer* do it for you. Check the Yellow Pages in the phone book. Or you may do it yourself with the *grid method.* Draw ¼" squares on your design (or a tracing-paper copy). Draw 1" squares on another piece of paper. Copy the lines inside each square, and you have just quadrupled the size of the original by yourself! By changing the size of the squares, you can vary the size of the final design (Figure 2-28a & b).

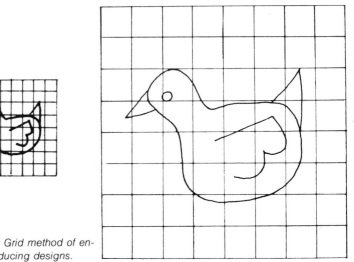

FIG. 2-28a & b *Grid method of enlarging and reducing designs.*

Transferring the design

Now that your design is the right size, it's easy to put it on canvas (Figure 2-29a–j). Use a *waterproof* grey marker to trace the outline of the design onto the canvas. Fill in with the appropriate colors. You may use acrylic paints instead of markers. Some additional suggestions for painting on canvas are:

Thin your paint with water to make it the same consistency as liquid dishwashing detergent. An eye dropper keeps you from adding too much water. It is better for the paint to be too thick than too thin. Ideally the paint should not clog the canvas holes nor should it come through on the other side of the canvas.

Use a broad, still brush for large areas and a finer, yet still stiff, one for smaller areas. Brushes that are too wet will dissolve the sizing on the canvas.

White (or tan) paint makes a good eraser. Cover your mistake with paint the same color as the canvas. Let it dry. Then you can paint right over it.

SUPPLIES AND BASIC PROCEDURES

Separate cans of water for each color save many trips to get clean water. Soup cans are ideal.

Mix paint in throw-away containers to make clean-up much easier. Yogurt containers and plastic egg cartons work well.

Clean-up with acrylic paints is easy—soap and water do the trick. But don't let the paint dry before you've cleaned the brushes.

Spray with a fixative to set the paint. Acrylic paint is permanent once it has dried. *But test it yourself.* Run it under water and blot with a white tissue.

Always allow at least 2″ margin and preferably a 3″ margin of blank canvas. This gives you room to hang onto for blocking and also room to change your mind.

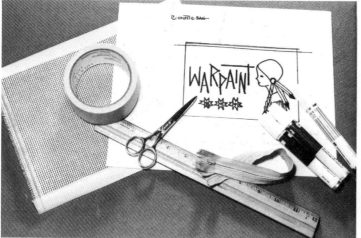

FIG. 2-29a (left) *Supplies needed to ready a canvas for stitching.*

FIG. 2-29b (below) *(1) canvas, (2) masking tape, (3) ruler, (4) scissors, (5) drawing of design, (6) zipper (used in this case to get correct size for a make-up bag), and (7) waterproof markers—if used instead of acrylic paints.*

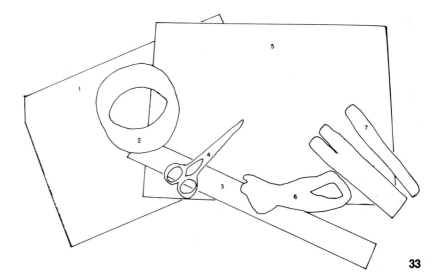

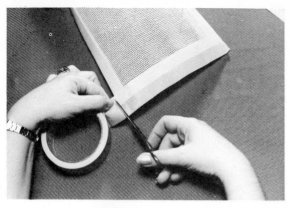

FIG. 2-29c *Bind the edges of the canvas with masking tape.*

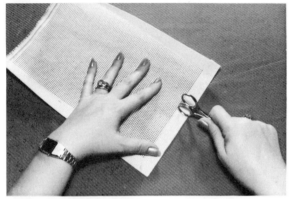

FIG. 2-29d *Rub the handle of a pair of scissors over the tape to make it stick better.*

FIG. 2-29e *Mark two of the margins with a waterproof marker.*

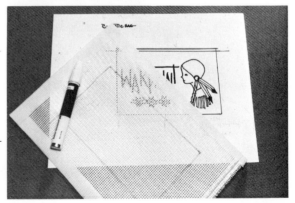

FIG. 2-29f *Trace your drawing with a black marker.*

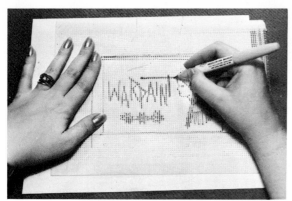

FIG. 2-29g *Lay the canvas over the design, and trace it onto the canvas with a waterproof grey marker.*

FIG. 2-29h *Your canvas should look like this.*

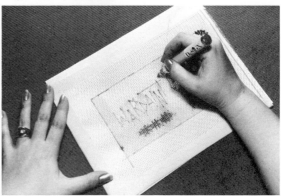

FIG. 2-29i *Paint the background. Let it dry.*

FIG. 2-29j *The canvas is now ready to stitch.*

Part I has introduced you to the supplies and basic procedures of needlepoint. Part II is next, and it holds the exciting key to *Needlepoint: The Third Dimension!*

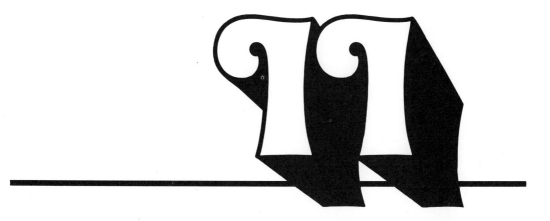

THE METHODS OF THREE-DIMENSIONAL NEEDLEPOINT

Chapter **3**

Two-dimensional needlepoint
that seems three-dimensional

In order to create a two-dimensional needlepoint piece that seems three-dimensional, you must create an optical illusion. This is done with color and line.

STITCHES: Basketweave
                     Continental (outline)

CANVAS: Penelope, Mono, or Interlock Mono 10, 11¼″ × 11½″ (3″ margin included)

YARN: Tapestry or Persian

NEEDLE: Size 18 or 20

SIZE OF FINISHED PROJECT: 5¼″ × 5½″

FIG. 3-1a *Stacked Cubes.*

Three shades of grey and black make these two basic shapes appear to be cubes, stacked one on top of another.

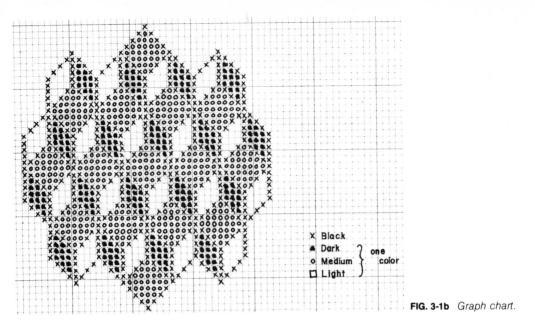

X	Black	
▲	Dark	one
○	Medium	color
□	Light	

FIG. 3-1b *Graph chart.*

This is a graphed design (Figure 3-1b). This means you begin with blank canvas. Fold your canvas in half and then in half again to find the center. Begin stitching from the center of the graph. Each X represents one Continental Stitch. (Figure 3-1c). Symbols are often used to indicate other colors. Each symbol is treated as if it were an X.

Stitch the outline first. Then fill in the other colors. When you have finished stitching, block (page 241) and frame (page 247).

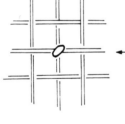

CONTINENTAL STITCH
ON
CANVAS

THIS EQUALS THIS

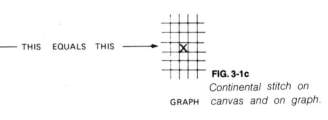

GRAPH

FIG. 3-1c
Continental stitch on canvas and on graph.

Ballet slippers

STITCHES: 1. Basketweave
2. Couching
3. Double Brick
Bargello (border)

THE METHODS OF THREE-DIMENSIONAL NEEDLEPOINT

CANVAS: Mono (Regular or Interlock) 14, x 22″ (3″ margins included)

YARN: Persian

NEEDLE: Size 20

SIZE OF FINISHED PROJECT. 16″ × 16″

The Bargello border here gives the feeling of ribbon that twists. It is emphasized by the real ribbon ties on the ballet slippers.

FIG. 3-2a *Ballet Slippers.*

Stitch the border first. It should be ½″ from the edge of the piece. Stitch both the slippers and the background before you lay the Couching thread for the outline of the slippers.

Block (page 241). Force the ends of the ribbon through the canvas where they are supposed to be attached to the shoes. Tack them in place with sewing thread. Curl the four pieces of ribbon (8″ to 9″ long) with a curling iron. Easy does it—don't burn the ribbon! Arrange the ribbon in a pleasing pattern. Hold in place with white glue. Frame as described on page 247.

FIG. 3-2b *Graph chart.*

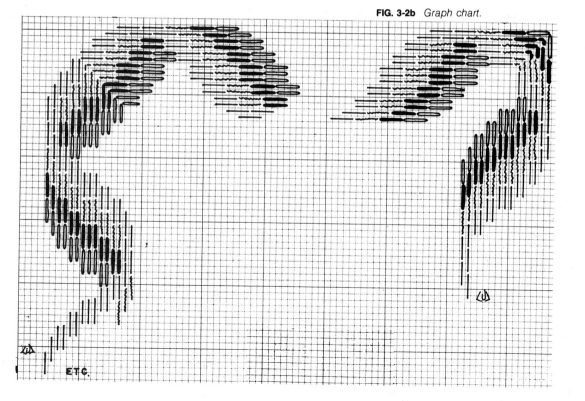

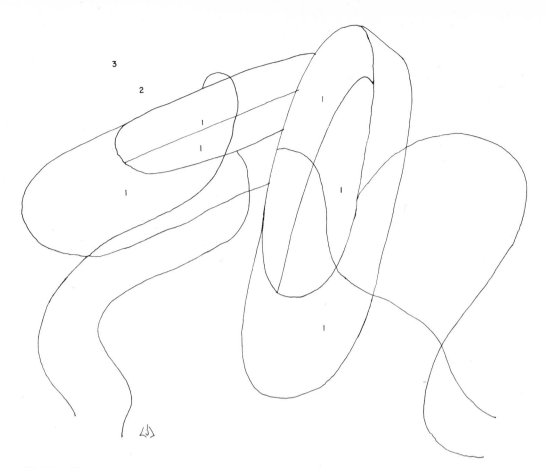

FIG. 3-2c *Slippers.*

FIG. 3-2d & e *Alphabets.*

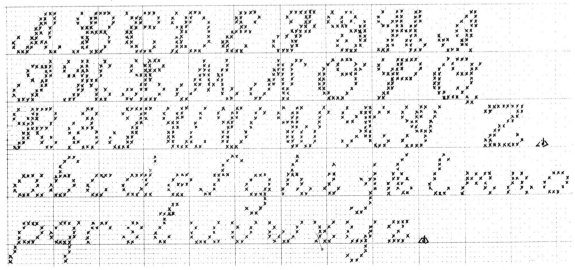

THE METHODS OF THREE-DIMENSIONAL NEEDLEPOINT

STITCHES: Giant Brick
            Backstitch (page 28)

CANVAS: Mono (Regular or Interlock) 18, 14¾" × 14¾"
(3" margins included)

YARN: Persian (2 ply—Mamma and Baby [or two Babies,
depending on your color]; see page 20).

NEEDLE: Size 22

SIZE OF FINISHED PROJECT: 8¾"× 8¾"

Color again creates the illusion that the cube has holes cut in
it. The mirror mat emphasizes the viewer's thought of illusion
and image.
    Stitch the design and background onto the canvas with
the Brick Stitch. Backstitch between color areas to make a
definite line. Use the darker of the two colors involved.
    Block (page 241), and frame (page 247).

FIG. 3-3a   *Three-Dimensional Cube.*

FIG. 3-3b   *Close-up.*

Two-dimensional needlepoint that seems three-dimensional

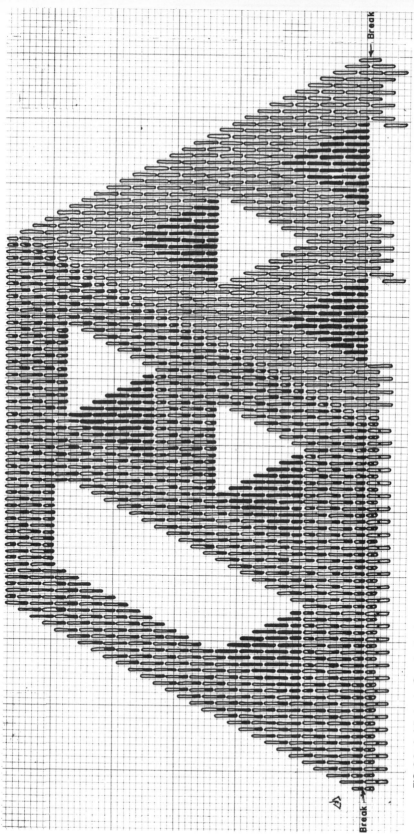

Break →

Break →

Break →

FIG. 3-3c & d (below) *Graph chart.*

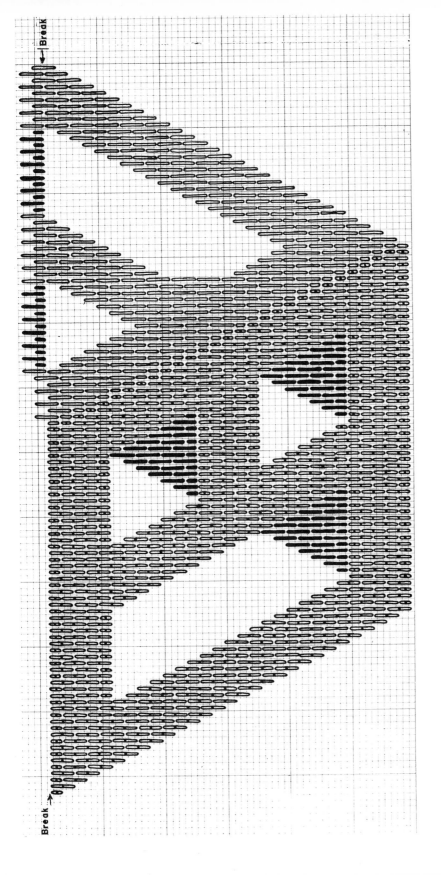

Break

Break

45

Triangle

STITCHES: Straight Stitches (see chart)
Backstitch (page 28)

CANVAS: Mono 18, 12″ x 12″ (3″ margins included)

YARN: Embroidery floss

NEEDLE: Size 22

SIZE OF FINISHED PROJECT: 6″ x 6″

Embroidery floss must be stripped just as yarn needs to be stripped. Unfortunately, my hint on stripping yarn does not apply to embroidery floss. Each ply needs to be pulled out completely. Then they all need to be put back together again.

Rolling the yarn is also important in working with embroidery floss. So, of course, a frame makes the whole process easier.

Again, use the Backstitch to delineate color areas as we did in the preceding project.

Block (page 241), and make into a pillow (page 253).

FIG. 3-4a *Triangle.*

FIG. 3-4b *Close-up.*

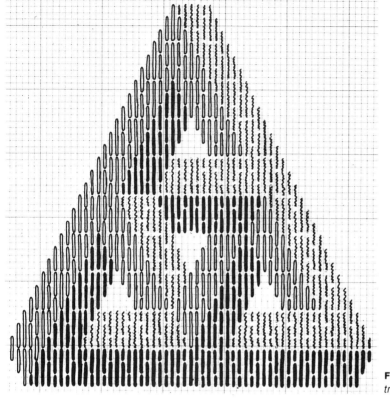

FIG. 3-4c *Graph chart, triangle.*

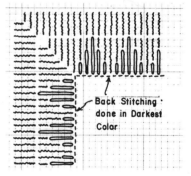

Back Stitching done in Darkest Color

FIG. 3-4d *Graph chart, border.*

4

Raised stitches

Raised Stitches give needlepoint some texture and thus, to a slight degree, a third dimension. Specific stitches raise the yarn from the surface of the canvas. You are probably already familiar with some of them: Turkey Work, Spider Webs, French Knots, etc. Others may be new to you. This chapter is merely an introduction to these stitches. Perhaps they will give you an idea how these stitches can be used and combined to give a different look to the same old designs.

Christmas wreath ornament

STITCHES: 1. Raised Buttonhole on a Raised Band
2. Mosaic
3. French Knot
4. Binding

CANVAS: Plastic 7, square 3″ × 3″

YARN: Persian

NEEDLE: Size 18

SIZE OF FINISHED PROJECT: 3″ × 3″

You'll have to fudge a bit in laying the Raised Band in a circle, but it isn't hard to do. Really pack the yarn in there. This wreath took about 20 yards of yarn. In working the Raised Buttonhole, push each row to the side, so you can get in as many rows as possible (see page 234). The more rows you get in, the fatter your wreath will be.

Next work the background. Then stitch the French Knots (berries) through the wreath. Braid yarn or crochet a chain for the hanger. Tack it to the back. (I inadvertently turned the canvas 90° when I attached the bow, berries, and hanger.) Glue or sew felt onto the back for a lining. (Don't iron a lining on—the plastic melts! How do you think I know the plastic melts?)

FIG. 4-1a *Christmas Wreath Ornament.*

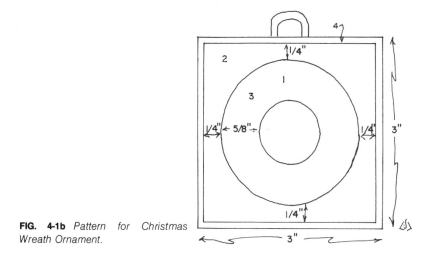

FIG. 4-1b *Pattern for Christmas Wreath Ornament.*

Black-eyed susan purse

STITCHES: 1. Looped Turkey Work
2. Giant Scotch
3. Needleweaving (petals)

CANVAS: Interlock Mono 10, 11″ × 11″ (2″ margins included)

YARN: Tapestry or Persian (Persian for Turkey Work), ribbon (for petals) (see page 13)

Raised stitches

49

FIG. 4-2a *Black-Eyed Susan purse.*

FIG. 4-2b *Close-up.*

NEEDLE: SIZE 18 or 20

SIZE OF FINISHED PROJECT: 7″ in diameter

Remember that painted wooden purse you have stashed on the top shelf of your closet? Revive it with a needlepoint top—or start anew.

The black-eyed Susan on the top was taken from the design on the sides.

Stitch the background first, leaving only a hole for the center of the flower. Then place the ribbon spokes so they radiate out from the center like petals. Use five lengthwise spokes for each flower. Place them as much like Figure 4-2c

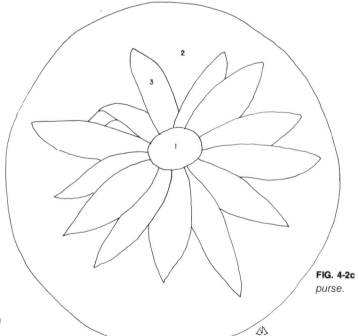

FIG. 4-2c *Pattern for Black-Eyed Susan purse.*

as you can. Stick two or three fingers under the ribbon as you lay the spokes. This will give each petal a poof. Exaggerate the poof, for some of it will be lost in the needleweaving. As you needleweave, keep the ribbon *smooth*.

Weave in a piece of wire on the underside of each petal. This will help keep the poof.

Stitch the Turkey Work last. Make it long and loopy. Separate the plies of the Persian yarn after you have stitched it. This makes it even loopier!

Block (page 241). When the needlepoint has dried, cut away the margin of canvas—right down to the stitching. Paint the little bits of canvas that remain with acrylic paints or a waterproof marker.

Glue the needlepoint to the top of the purse. Trim the edge with a twisted cord (page 255). Mine is made from six strands of yarn.

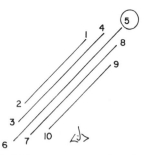

FIG. 4-2d *Arrangement of spokes for petals.*

Apple tree mirror

STITCHES: 1. Basketweave
               2. Spider Web
               3. Raised Close Herringbone
               4. Raised Buttonhole on a Raised Band

CANVAS: Interlock Mono 12, 11″ × 16¾″ (2″ margins included)

YARN: Tapestry or Persian (bark and sky)
           Pearl cotton (apples and leaves)

NEEDLE: Size 20

SIZE OF FINISHED PROJECT: 7″ × 12¾″

Pearl cotton loses its sheen easily. Work with a shorter thread, and handle it gently. Don't manhandle your piece while you're working on it. Don't let the worked areas of pearl cotton rub against anything.

Because pearl cotton doesn't have the body of wool, the apples will have to be helped along. Pack the pearl cotton in as you stitch the apples. Keep pulling the thread to the center after every stitch you take. The apples still will not be rounded. So stuff them with polyester fiber. Poke it in gently

FIG. 4-3a *Apple Tree Mirror.*

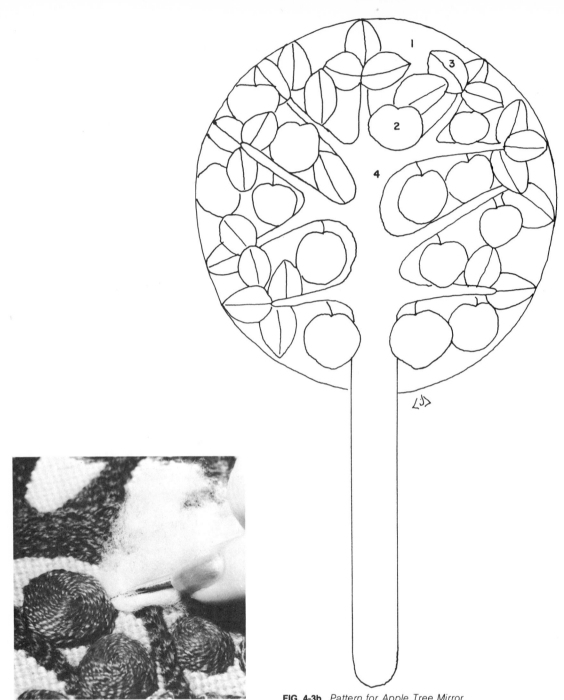

FIG. 4-3b *Pattern for Apple Tree Mirror.*

FIG. 4-3c *Stuffing the apples.*

between the stitches with the points of embroidery scissors (Figure 4-3c). Block (page 241).

Have a carpenter build you a frame, or order it from the source listed on page 262.

STITCHES: Double Leviathan
                   Half Cross
                   Smyrna Cross
                   2 × 2 Slanted Gobelin

CANVAS: Interlock Mono 12 (see Figure 4-4b)

YARN: Tapestry or Persian, five colors used

NEEDLE: Size 20

SIZE OF FINISHED PROJECT: 4″ × 4″ × 2¾″

Each of the four sides of the box is stitched on one long strip of canvas. Leave one mesh between these sides. Work Half Cross Stitch along this mesh. Also work Half Cross all the way around the four sides like a picture frame. When the box is assembled, these rows of Half Cross will be the corners. Work the box top on a separate piece of canvas. The bottom is a piece of mat board the same size as the top. It will not be stitched but covered, instead, with a piece of felt.

     Accurate counting is very important in the construction of this box. If you're off 1 mesh, the box will not go together smoothly.

     See Figure 4-4a–g for the charts to guide you in stitching each of the sides and the top. It's easier to stitch if you start in the center of each piece and work out. The pattern is

FIG. 4-4a *Jody's Needlepoint Box.*

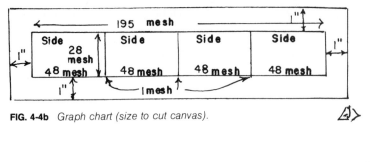

FIG. 4-4b *Graph chart (size to cut canvas).*

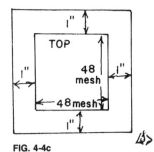

FIG. 4-4c

FIG. 4-4d

1. AQUA	DC-SMYRNA
2. LT. AQUA	DL-DOUBLE LEVIATHAN
3. RED VIOLET	HC-HALF CROSS
4. ORANGE	
5. LT. ORANGE	

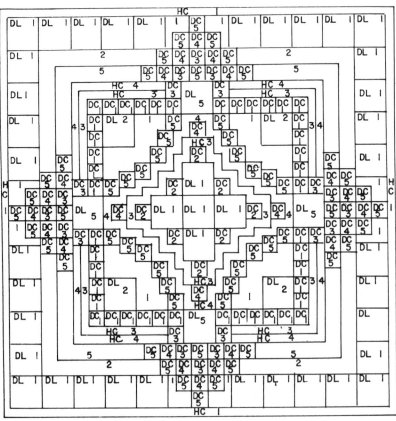

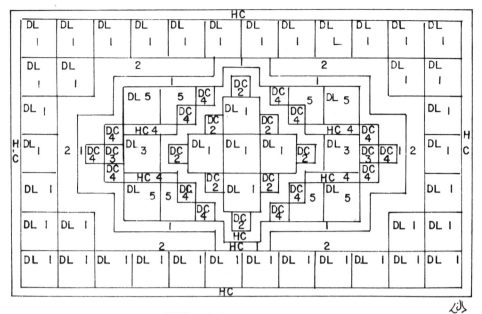

SIDE — (4)

FIG. 4-4e

FIG. 4-4f

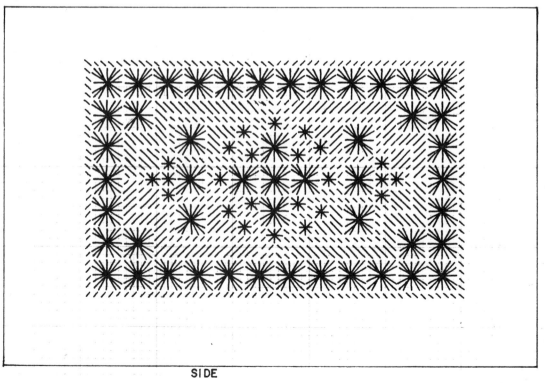

SIDE

Raised stitches

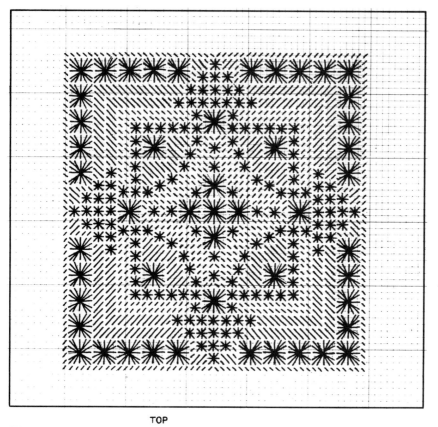

TOP

FIG. 4-4g

symmetrical. All diagonal stitches are slanted from the corners toward the center. Check the diagrams.

Block (page 241) and finish according to the instructions on page 257.

Hint: Choose the lining fabric first and then the yarn. It's easier to match this way.

Four seasons bell pull

STITCHES: 1. Cut Turkey
2. Woven Spider Web
3. Wound Cross
4. Cross
5. French Knots

6. Close Herringbone
7. Backstitch
8. French Knots on Stalks
9. Mosaic (Reversed Mosaic better)
10. Smooth Spider Web
11. Raised Rope
12. Diamond Ray
13. Couching
14. Chain
15. Boullion Knots

CANVAS: Mono (Regular or Interlock) 10, 4¼″ × 17¼″

YARN: Tapestry or Persian

NEEDLE: Size 18 or 20

SIZE OF FINISHED PROJECT: 3″ × 16″

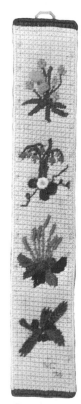

Stitches are used here to create things we associate with the four seasons. Improvise to get the effect you wish, particularly with the Leaf Stitch.

Using the Two-Step Edge-Finishing Method allows us to finish a raw edge of canvas as we stitch. The project must be planned before you take the first stitch, however; this method also prepares the canvas for the Binding Stitch.

On Mono canvas you need just 6 mesh all the way around your design. Figure 4-5c will show you where those 6 mesh are. On a bell pull that uses hardware to hang from, these instructions apply only to the sides (see Figure 4-5d). You will need 3″ of canvas at either end to attach the bell pull hardware. This bell pull has all four sides finished with the Two-Step Edge-Finishing Method. Sew a hanger on the back.

Insert your needle under the 5th and 6th mesh. Fold the canvas so that these two mesh are on the edge and so that there will be a 4-mesh hem (Figure 4-5). If you wish to baste the hem in place, do so now. Be sure the mesh line up. Stitch through both thicknesses of the canvas as if they were one. Only the 2-mesh edge for the Binding Stitch should show (Figure 4-5f). See also the photo in the section about the Binding Stitch (page 198).

Follow the directions for blocking with T-pins on page 243. Slip the ends of blank canvas through the slot for them on your bell pull hardware. Sew the hem down. Line as explained on page 257.

FIG. 4-5a *Four Seasons Bell Pull.*

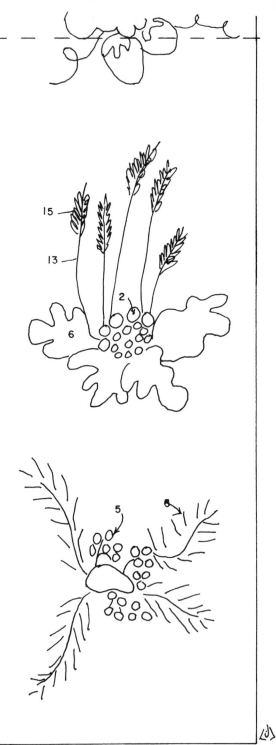

FIG. 4-5b *Pattern for Four Seasons Bell Pull.*

THE METHODS OF THREE-DIMENSIONAL NEEDLEPOINT

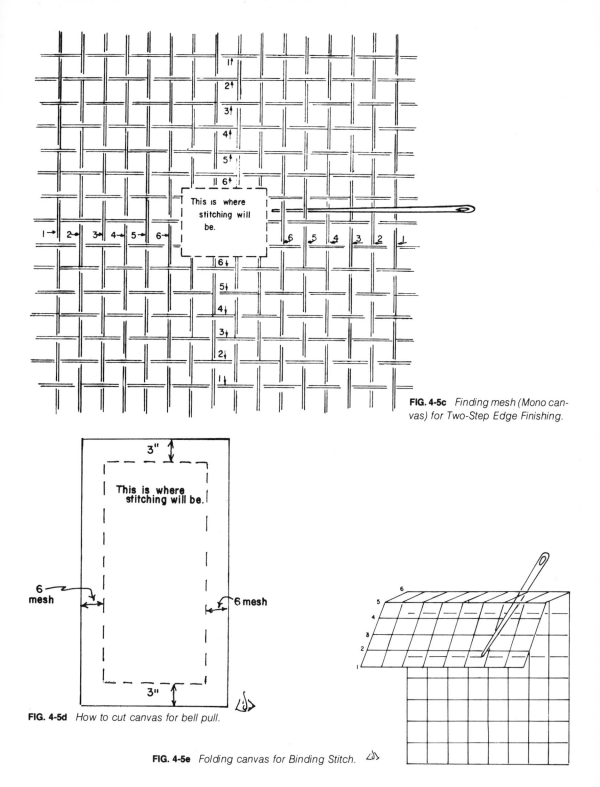

FIG. 4-5c *Finding mesh (Mono canvas) for Two-Step Edge Finishing.*

This is where
stitching will
be.

This is where
stitching will be.

3"

6
mesh

6 mesh

3"

FIG. 4-5d *How to cut canvas for bell pull.*

FIG. 4-5e *Folding canvas for Binding Stitch.*

Raised stitches

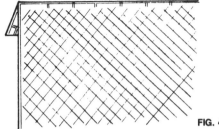

FIG. 4-5f *Stitch right up to edge.*

FIG. 4-5g *Spring close-up.*

FIG. 4-5h *Summer close-up.*

FIG. 4-5i *Fall close-up.*

FIG. 4-5j *Winter close-up.*

THE METHODS OF THREE-DIMENSIONAL NEEDLEPOINT

STITCHES:
1. Smyrna Cross
2. Double Straight Cross
3. Bullion Knots
4. French Knots on Stalks
5. Cut Turkey Work
6. French Knots
7. Double Straight Cross
8. Ray (all leaves)
9. Needleweaving
10. Smooth Spider Web
11. Looped Turkey Work
12. Raised Rope
13. Woven Spider Web
14. Ridged Spider Web
15. Starfish
16. Wound Cross
17. Basketweave

CANVAS: Mono (Regular or Interlock) 10 (see Figure 4-6b for pattern)

YARN: Tapestry or Persian

NEEDLE: Size 18 or 20

SIZE OF FINISHED PROJECT: 8" × 4½"

FIG. 4-6a *Scissors Case.*

This scissors case gives you an opportunity to play with all kinds of neat, bumpy stitches! The stitches and their placement are only a guideline for you. Play with the stitches, and create a bouquet of flowers of your own! Hint: Vary the length of the French Knots on Stalks for more interesting flowers.

The finishing of the raw canvas edge is, in theory, the Two-Step Edge-Finishing Method (page 57). However, because the whole piece of canvas is not on the straight grain of the canvas, you'll have to fudge a bit. On those sides of canvas not cut on the straight grain, cut the margin of canvas the width of 6 mesh. Turn it under, leaving something to put the Binding Stitch on. Stitch through both thicknesses of canvas as best you can. But be sure that the size and tension of the stitches on the right side is uniform.

Stitch more flowers on the other side, put on a monogram, or do your own thing. But have fun!

Raised stitches

FIG. 4-6b *Pattern for Scissors Case.*

Block (page 241) and line (page 257). Sew the seam with the Binding Stitch, and continue it around the top edge to finish it off.

STITCHES:
1. Diagonal Cashmere
2. Couching
3. Interlocking Gobelin
4. Looped Turkey Work
5. Petit Point
6. Byzantine #3 (reversed)
7. Continental (stems)
8. Raised Buttonhole on Raised Band
9. French Knot
10. French Knot on Stalks
11. Ridged Spider Web
12. Raised Rope
13. Raised Cup
14. Wound Cross
15. Raised Close Herringbone
16. Cut Turkey Work
17. 2 × 2 Cross
18. Straight Stitches
19. Plaited Herringbone
20. Close Herringbone
21. Knotted Stitch
22. Ray
23. Thorn
24. Bullion Knots
25. Needleweaving
26. Starfish

FIG. 4-7a *Farm.*

CANVAS: Penelope 10, 18″ × 22″ (3″ margins included)

YARN: Tapestry or Persian

NEEDLE: Size 18 or 20, size 22 for Petit Point

SIZE OF FINISHED PROJECT: 12″ × 16″

This farm is yet another opportunity to play with stitches to get the desired effect.

Split the mesh of the Penelope canvas so that you will be able to stitch the barn and wagon in Petit Point. The fence takes a little maneuvering to put the Plaited Herringbone at an angle.

FIG. 4-7b–h *Close-ups.*
FIG. 4-7b

Raised stitches

FIG. 4-7c

FIG. 4-7d

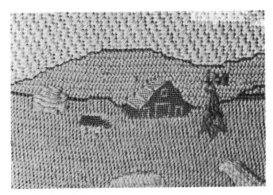

FIG. 4-7e

FIG. 4-7f

FIG. 4-7g

FIG. 4-7h

THE METHODS OF THREE-DIMENSIONAL NEEDLEPOINT

FIG. 4-7i *Pattern for Farm.*

Raised stitches

This piece is difficult to get straight in blocking. Persevere; it can be straight! It will help to work on a frame. If you don't usually use one, I strongly suggest that you try one. This project is a good place to start.

Do all surface stitchery after blocking. Frame as shown on page 247.

5

Needlepoint in the round

Needlepoint in the round gives us an opportunity to make things out of needlepoint that were otherwise unheard-of in stitchery. Plastic canvas is largely responsible for this opportunity. Included in this chapter are merely ideas to spur you on to projects of your own.

Basket of flowers

STITCHES: 1. Mosaic
               2. Scotch
               3. Byzantine
               4. Buttonhole

CANVAS: Plastic 10. Each of the six flowers takes a piece of canvas about 6″ × 6″. So if you have to buy the canvas rather than work from scraps, buy just 6 inches, 36″ wide. However, this is a perfect project to use scrap canvas on. Only a ⅛″ margin is needed.

YARN: Tapestry or Persian (flowers)
            Velour (leaves)

FIG. 5-1a *Basket of Flowers.*

NEEDLE: Size 18 or 20, crewel needle for Buttonhole Stitch

SIZE OF FINISHED PROJECT: Six flowers fill a basket 7″ in diameter. Each flower alone is about 5″ wide—plus the leaves.

This is a nice project for beginners. Neither the stitching nor the assembly of the flowers is difficult.

Stitch six petals for each flower and two leaves per flower. Cut each leaf and petal out—right down to the stitching. Leave an unstitched tab as indicated on the drawing. Glue fabric to the backs of each of the pieces. Trim to the stitching. Allow them to dry. Using a crewel needle, work the Buttonhole Stitch to bind the edge of the canvas and to attach the wire (Figure 5-1c). Do not get blood on your needlepoint.

Assemble the flower as shown in Figure 5-1d–f.

Glue Styrofoam into the bottom of a basket or other vessel. Weight it down, and allow it to dry *thoroughly*. Note: Special glue, available at craft stores, is needed for Styrofoam. Other glues dissolve the Styrofoam.

Arrange the flowers in the basket. Make a bow, and attach it to the handle of the basket. If making bows isn't your thing, buy a bow, or ask a florist to make one for you.

FIG. 5-1c *Binding edge of canvas.*

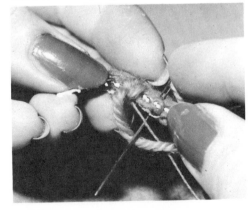

FIG. 5-1b *Pattern for petals and leaves.*

THE METHODS OF THREE-DIMENSIONAL NEEDLEPOINT

FIG. 5-1d *Materials needed for assembling flower.*

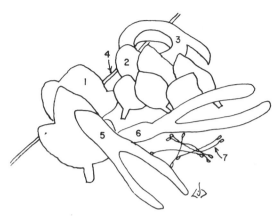

FIG. 5-1e *(1) Two needlepoint leaves, (2) six needlepoint petals, (3) florist tape, (4) medium-weight florist wire, (5) pliers, (6) needle-nose pliers, and (7) stamen (from craft store).*

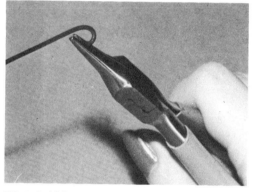

FIG. 5-1f *Make a small loop with needle-nose pliers.*

FIG. 5-1g *Fold a bunch of stamens in half, and insert them into the loop.*

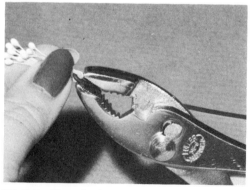

FIG. 5-1h *Close the loop.*

FIG. 5-1i *Cover the wire loop and about ¼" of stamen with florist tape. Position the first petal.*

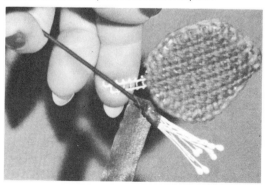

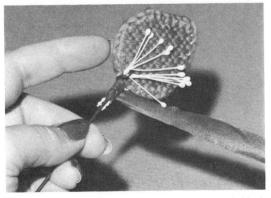

FIG. 5-1j *Tape the petal in place (through hindsight, I discovered the stamen should be taped ¼" up!).*

FIG. 5-1k *Tape the three small petals in a triangular arrangement.*

FIG. 5-1l *Tape the three large petals in a triangular arrangement around the three smaller ones.*

FIG. 5-1m *Tape the two leaves farther down the wire stem. Tape the rest of the stem.*

FIG. 5-1n *Shape the petals by folding the sides up.*

FIG. 5-1o *Then bend the tip of the petal back.*

STITCHES: 1. Leaf #1
2. F-106
3. Slanted Gobelin
4. Tied Windmill
Binding

CANVAS: Plastic canvas: drum—2" circle (two); Plastic 10, 10" × 26 mesh (for tall drum) or 10" × 20 mesh (for shorter drum); Christmas tree—7" × 7" × 6½"; Plastic 10 (cut three); tree base—6½" × 6½" × 6½"; package—3" square (six).

YARN: Persian, metallics (silver and gold) for trim

NEEDLE: Size 16

SIZE OF FINISHED PROJECT: Tree—7" × 7" × 6½"; package—3" × 3" × 3"; drum—3" × 3⅝"

Because plastic canvas is so rigid, it is good for items such as these. Cut a sheet of plastic canvas to the shapes specified above. When you cut, be sure to cut the canvas so that there are smooth edges (Figure 5-2d). When you stitch, be sure the yarn covers the canvas. Thicken as necessary.

FIG. 5-2a *Christmas Mobile.*

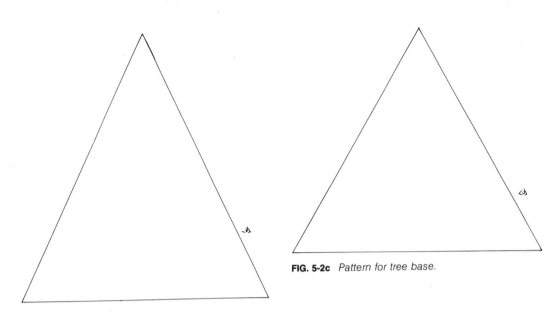

FIG. 5-2b *Pattern for tree.*

FIG. 5-2c *Pattern for tree base.*

FIG. 5-2d *How to cut plastic canvas.*

WRONG   **RIGHT**

Stitch the sides of the drum in F-106. Reverse the pattern for the top and bottom rows. Stitch the top in Slanted Gobelin. Put the drum together with an Overcast Stitch. Decorate the center section of the drum with a gold metallic thread. Put toy drumsticks on the top with white glue. Can't find any drumsticks? Carve your own from a ¼″ dowel. Not as hard as you might think! Sand and stain them.

Stitch four Tied Windmills on each of the six package pieces. Work the Slanted Gobelin around them. Put the package together with an Overcast Stitch. Tie it with a metallic thread.

It might be easier to get the tree the right size if you stitch it first and then cut it out. The top row has one Leaf Stitch, and the bottom row has six leaves. Decorate each of the three sides of the tree with colored glass beads (for ornaments) and a metallic thread (for the garland). Put the tree together with a Binding Stitch. Make a star for the top from two large gold sequins.

Use fishing line to hang the ornaments. Attach the other end of the fishing line to one of several kinds of hangers. Use your imagination.

THE METHODS OF THREE-DIMENSIONAL NEEDLEPOINT

STITCHES: Basketweave

CANVAS: Silk gauze, 54 mesh per inch, 1½″ × 1½″

YARN: 1 strand variegated embroidery floss

NEEDLE: Fine sewing needle

SIZE OF FINISHED PROJECT: 1″ × ½″ × ⅜″

FIG. 5-3a *Bird Necklace.*

Get out your magnifying glass, and give silk gauze a try. It makes beautiful tiny things. You probably can see it without a magnifying glass, but it sure helps to have it.

The variegated thread on the 54 gauge gives a nice repeat pattern on the colors. You could use a silk gauze with 40 mesh per inch rather than 54, but the repeat pattern of the colors is not so frequent.

Stitch the bird. Apply a *light* coating of glue to the back of your stitches. Take care that the glue does not soak through. Be sure to get the glue on the edges. Let the glue dry. Cut the bird out—very carefully. Starting at the head, whip the seams together with one ply of the variegated embroidery floss. Stitch to the tip of the tail. Then attach the wings with a Backstitch—right through both thicknesses of canvas. Attach a ½″ loop of *nylon* thread through the body and center of the wings. This loop is to hang the bird in the cage.

Continue to stitch the rest of the seams together, leaving a hole big enough for the points of embroidery scissors to go through. Stuff with polyester fiber. Finish sewing the seam.

Use your bird any way you like—or order the cage shown here from the source listed on page 261.

FIG. 5-3b *Pattern for bird.*

Actual Size

Airplane

FIG. 5-4a *Airplane.*

STITCHES: 1. Basketweave
2. Continental
3. Straight Gobelin
4. Backstitch (page 28)
5. Double Stitch
6. Interlocking Gobelin
7. Straight Stitch
8. Smooth Spider Web
   Binding Stitch

CANVAS: Plastic 5, see Figure 5-4b

YARN: Persian

NEEDLE: Size 13

SIZE OF FINISHED PROJECT: 22″ × 23″ × 9½″ (You can make it virtually any size you would like.)

Transfer the pattern to the canvas by tracing. Use a water-proof marker. Some brands do not work well on plastic canvas, or they rub off once you do get it on. You will have to experiment. Paint chips off.

Stitch according to the patterns in Figure 5-4b & c. On plastic canvas, it doesn't matter which direction you pick for the straight grain. But once you do, follow the straight grain lines religiously. If you don't, when it comes time to put the pieces together, they won't go together easily. Then cut out the pieces as shown in Figure 5-4c. Leave a 1-mesh margin for assembly.

Put the engines together by folding them like Figure 5-4d. Slash the canvas to the X. Overlap the 1 blank mesh. Stitch, continuing Interlocking Gobelin. Whip circles of blank canvas onto both ends of the engine (Figure 5-4d). Carefully burying your tails (with a Bargello Tuck, page 23) on the right side of the engine, work a Smooth Spider Web over the circle of blank canvas. Make it as round and high as you can. Cut your yarn long enough to make the whole Smooth Spider Web, because it is a pain in the neck to bury the tails.

Using a Whipstitch, attach the engines to the under-wing on the spots marked. It's almost impossible to get all four engines parallel and straight, but you might as well try anyway!

Join the wings with the Binding Stitch. Then, using a Whipstitch again, attach the wings to the body of the plane.

Sew the tailpieces A and B together with the Binding Stitch. Attach tailpieces B to the plane, just as you did the wings. Hold off for a minute on tailpiece A.

Cut a piece of canvas 3 mesh by 12". Use this piece to assemble the nose of the plane. Start on the belly of the plane—where the line separates to form the nose. Stitch the long piece to the plane as shown in Figure 5-4e & f. Stitch 1 edge mesh of the long piece to one side of the plane, and stitch the other edge mesh of the long piece to the other side of the plane. Stitch the middle mesh. Try to follow the stitch and color pattern as best you can. You will truly wish you had an extra hand, but it can be done. Trust me. Continue with the extra piece to the top of the plane—at least to where the color changes from blue to grey.

These shenanigans you just went through give your plane a somewhat rounded nose.

FIG. 5-4b *Patterns for airplane wings and tail.*

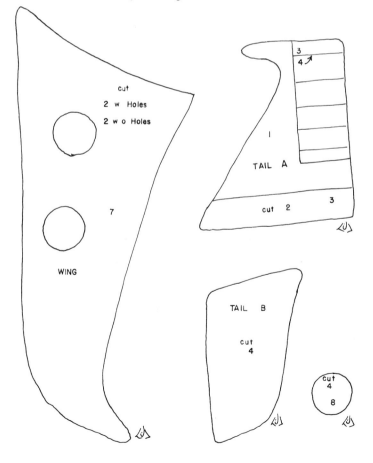

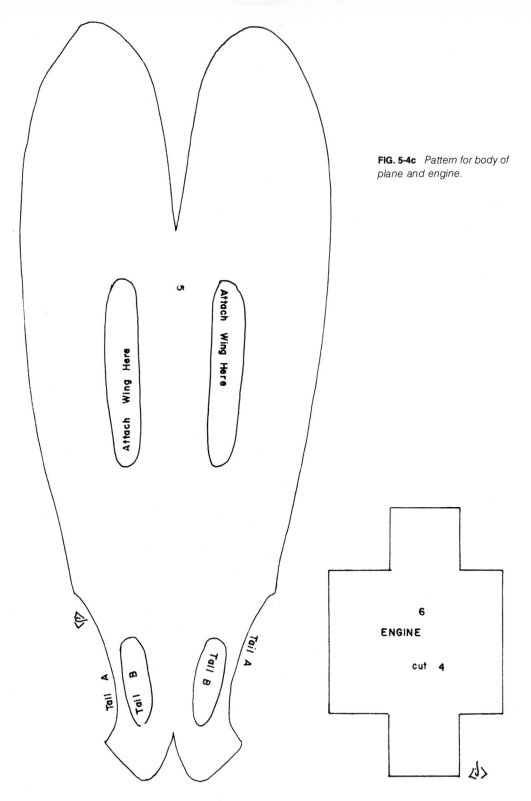

FIG. 5-4c *Pattern for body of plane and engine.*

THE METHODS OF THREE-DIMENSIONAL NEEDLEPOINT

Continue sewing the top seam of the airplane—just as you did on the engine. When you come to the place where tailpiece A fits, split the seam, and attach the right side of tailpiece A to the right side of the plane. Sew the left side of tailpiece A to the left side of the plane. Use an Overcast Stitch to do this.

Finish sewing the body together with the Binding Stitch. Don't forget to change colors as the plane's color pattern changes. The plane needs no stuffing.

Hang the plane from the ceiling with fishing line.

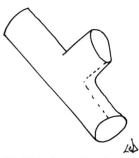

FIG. 5-4d *Assembly of engine.*

FIG. 5-4e & f (below) *Assembly of plane.*

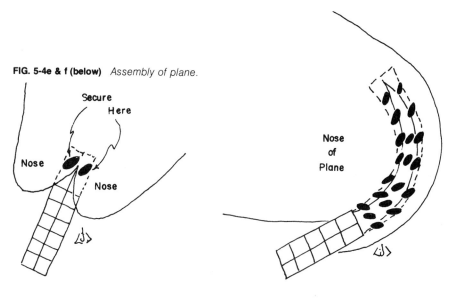

Golf cart

STITCHES: 1. Mosaic
                2. Basketweave
                3. Continental
                4. Cut Turkey Work
                5. Diagonal Cashmere
                   Binding

CANVAS: Cart—Plastic 7 (see Figure 5-5b for canvas-cutting instructions); canopy—2″ to 3″ squares of Plastic canvas with raised center; base—Plastic 10, 10″ x 12″; sides of base—10″ x 1″ (cut two) and 12″ x 1″ (cut two)

YARN: Persian

Needlepoint in the round

FIG. 5-5a *Golf Cart.*

FIG. 5-5b *Patterns for Golf Cart.*

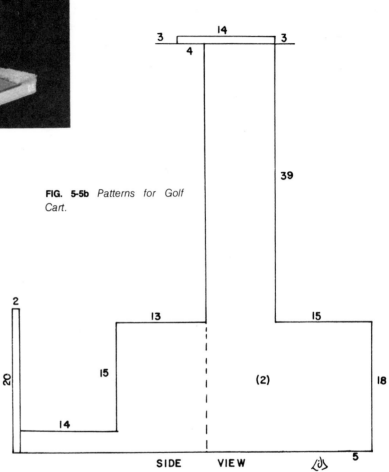

3　　14　　3

4

39

2

20

13　　　　15

15　　　　　(2)　　　18

14

5

SIDE　　VIEW

FRONT END - BACK END

1"　　　　(2)

10"

FRONT SIDE - BACK SIDE

1"　　　　(2)

12"

　　　THE METHODS OF THREE-DIMENSIONAL NEEDLEPOINT

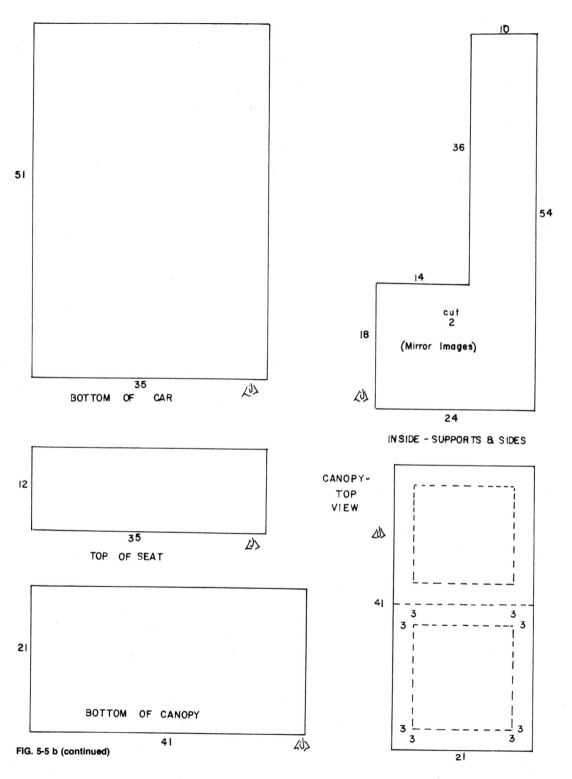

51

35

BOTTOM OF CAR

10

36

54

14

cut
2

(Mirror Images)

18

24

INSIDE - SUPPORTS & SIDES

12

35

TOP OF SEAT

CANOPY-
TOP
VIEW

41

3   3
3   3

3   3
3   3

21

21

BOTTOM OF CANOPY

41

FIG. 5-5 b (continued)

79

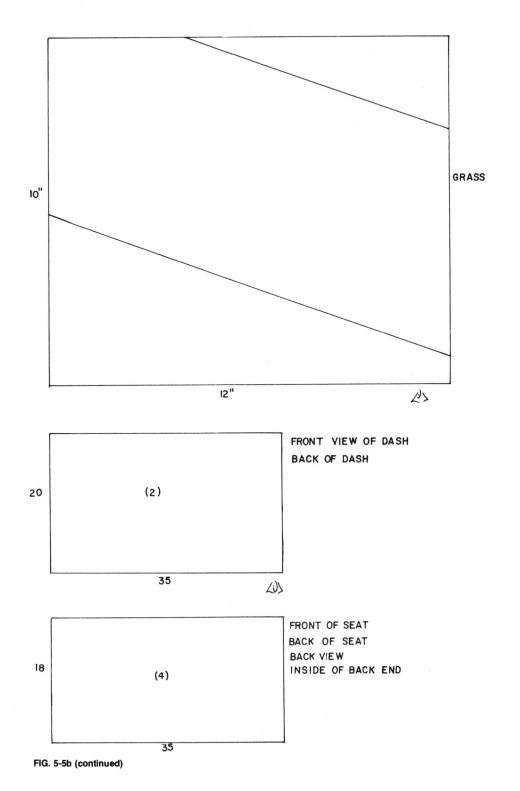

10"

12"

GRASS

FRONT VIEW OF DASH
BACK OF DASH

20

(2)

35

18

(4)

FRONT OF SEAT
BACK OF SEAT
BACK VIEW
INSIDE OF BACK END

35

FIG. 5-5b (continued)

THE METHODS OF THREE-DIMENSIONAL NEEDLEPOINT

NEEDLE: Size 16

SIZE OF FINISHED PROJECT: 12″ × 10″ × 11½″

Cut and stitch the canvas pieces as shown in Figure 5-5b. If you cannot get the squares of plastic canvas with the raised center (for the roof) (Figure 5-5c), just cut the top of the canopy the same size as the bottom. Use the alphabet in Figure 5-5d to stitch a name or initials on the front of the cart. Use the alphabet in Figure 5-5c to stitch "World's Greatest Golfer," your initials, and the date on the base.

FIG. 5-5c   *Plastic square for roof.*

Put the cart and the base together with the Binding Stitch.

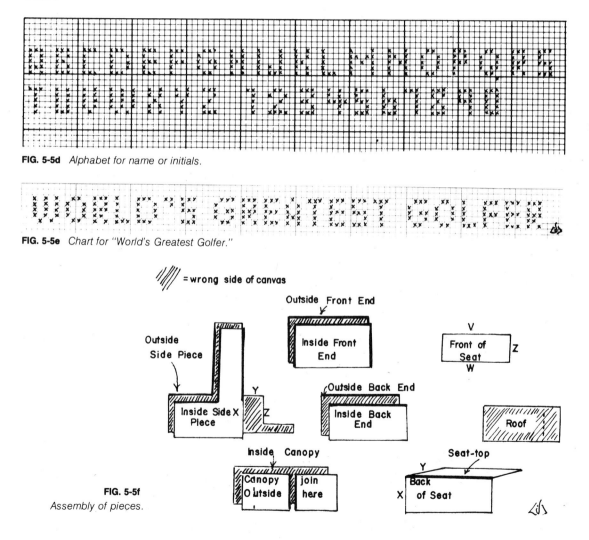

FIG. 5-5d   *Alphabet for name or initials.*

FIG. 5-5e   *Chart for "World's Greatest Golfer."*

FIG. 5-5g *Sew together with Binding Stitch.*

FIG. 5-5h *Rubber things for fingers.*

The cart needs to be assembled in the following order: First stitch the inside of the side pieces to the outsides of the same pieces (see Figure 5-5e). Bind along the heavy black lines *only*—for right now. Even though the drawings and instructions are shown for one side, repeat the instructions for the other side of the cart.

When that's done, bind the back of the seat to the side pieces along the line marked X. Join the two back end pieces (already together) to the side pieces. Your Binding Stitch will go through four thicknesses of canvas at the corners. If you have trouble getting the needle through, put those rubber thimblelike things that secretaries use on your thumb and index finger (Figure 5-5g). (Be sure to buy two different sizes!) Now the needle will be easy to pull.

Next attach the bottom of the cart. Stitch along both sides and across the back end. Sew the back of the seat to the bottom of the cart. Be sure the right side is up.

Now sew the rest of the seat in place—along seams V, W, Y, and Z.

Join the front end to the bottom of the cart and up the sides for those 2 or 3 mesh.

Attach the roof supports to the bottom of the roof along the dotted lines as in Figure 5-5e. Put the roof top on now. Using one ply of yarn, baste the two pieces together with a Backstitch. It's too bulky to bind and then put fringe on. Use a Whipstitch to cover the canvas at every other hole. The fringe will go in the empty holes.

Next, fringe the top with a yarn that is two ply white and one ply red. Make the fringe according to Figure 5-5j.

FIG. 5-5i *Pieces of cart—ready to be put together.*

THE METHODS OF THREE-DIMENSIONAL NEEDLEPOINT

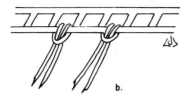

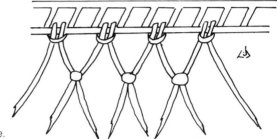

FIG. 5-5j *Making fringe.*

Buy 1½" wheels, hubcaps, and 6" axles from a hobby shop. With a Whipstitch, sew the axles (with the wheels attached) to the bottom of the cart.

Buy a 9" or 10" doll from a toy store for your golfer. The golf bag and clubs come from a cake-decorating supply store. The ball is a hat pin with a pearl on the end.

Cut a 1"-thick piece of Styrofoam a hair bigger than the base. Place the base over it. It should be a snug fit. Cut the hat pin, so that it is about ¾" long. Push it through the needlepoint, into the Styrofoam.

Using lightweight wire, attach the cart to the path on the base. Wire the golfer to the grass. Wire right through the Styrofoam. Give the wire a few twists to hold it in place.

Glue felt to the bottom, and you have a unique and personal gift!

6

Detached canvas

Oftentimes a portion of a design will lend itself to a three-dimensional look. The detached canvas method can give added depth to the petals of a flower, the wings of a bird or angel, leaves, etc.

This technique can be used to focus attention on a certain portion of a design. The detached canvas method can be used to make near things seem closer, thus making faraway things recede. See the Bulletin Board on page 88. Or it can make things seem more real, as in the case of the wreath (below) or the House (page 101).

Christmas wreath

STITCHES: Reversed Scotch (leaves)
Continental (outline)
Basketweave (background)
Buttonhole (edge) background and leaf edges

CANVAS: Interlock Mono 10, 21″ × 21″ (3″ margins included); leaves—approximately 19″ × 19″ (½″ margins included)

YARN: Tapestry or Persian (about 4 oz. of three greens)

NEEDLE: Size 18 or 20 crewel needle

SIZE OF FINISHED PROJECT: 16" in diameter

Transfer the pattern of the background to the piece of canvas 21" × 21". Arrange the three leaf patterns on the other piece of canvas. Squeeze them on any way they'll fit. (You only need a ¼" margin.) You'll want them to go in different directions. Turn the three leaf patterns over, so that you now have six patterns to use. By the time they get stitched, each one will be a little different, and you will have a nice variety of shapes. Make six leaves of each of the six shapes. Stitch a total of thirty-six separate leaves. Paint the canvas (page 32). Then stitch the leaves and the background canvas in three shades of green. Outline each separate leaf and each leaf on the background piece in the darkest color. Also stitch the vein in the darkest green. Stitch the insides of all the leaves in the lightest shade of green. Fill in the background in the medium shade of green.

The squares on the background canvas should be left blank. Leave the triangles and the leaf tabs blank, too. The leaves will be attached to the squares later. The Christmas tree lights (which will be the berries) will go through the triangles.

When all the stitching is finished, block both pieces of canvas (page 241). Next, *lightly* glue a fabric lining to the

FIG. 6-1a *Christmas Wreath.*

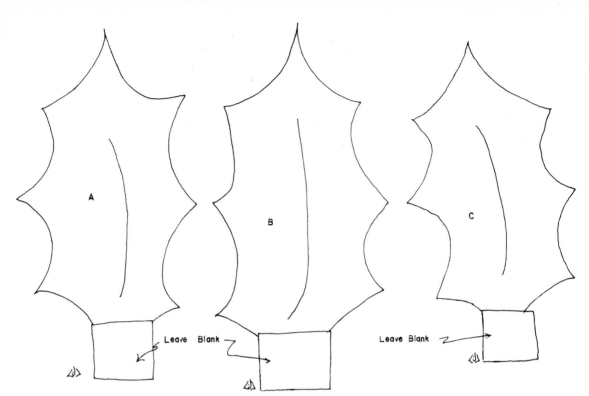

A

B

C

Leave Blank

Leave Blank

FIG. 6-1b *Pattern for wreath.*

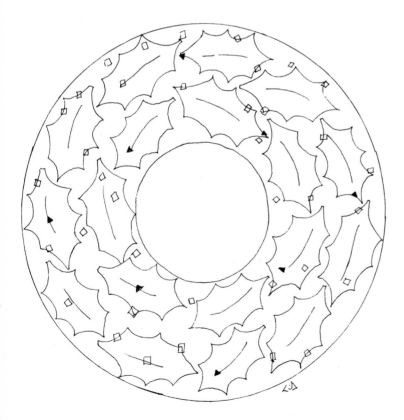

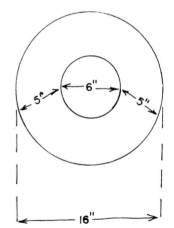

5" — 6" — 5"

16"

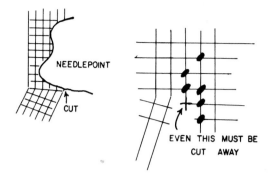

NEEDLEPOINT

CUT

EVEN THIS MUST BE
CUT AWAY

FIG. 6-1c & d *How to cut out leaves.*

backs of each of the leaves. Be sure the glue is on all edges of stitching. Mary used a bright red and white striped polyester and cotton fabric. You'll need about a quarter of a yard. When the glue dries, cut out each leaf—lining, too—right down to the needlepoint stitches. See Figure 6-1c–d. You won't need a tab of fabric (just canvas), so cut the lining off at the stitching. Keep the canvas tab.

Wiring the edges allows you to shape the leaves any way you wish. Attach a lightweight wire with the Buttonhole Stitch in the darkest color (see Figure 5-1c). Use a crewel needle to pierce the fabric.

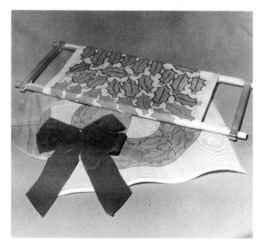

FIG. 6-1e *Positioning leaves.*

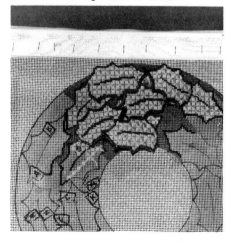

FIG. 6-1f *Stitching leaves on canvas.*

FIG. 6-1g *Close-up.*

To secure the leaves to the background canvas, lay the tab of the leaf over the square of blank canvas on the background canvas. Match the mesh as best you can. Cut the tab to the size of the square on the background canvas. Stitch through both thicknesses of canvas as if they were one. Continue with the same stitch that surrounds the tab.

Cut out the triangles of blank canvas. Glue the edges. Work the Buttonhole Stitch around the edge for added strength.

Finally, take a green marker or green paint, and paint any canvas that shows. (It's called cheating—don't tell!) Finish the wreath as described on page 259.

Bulletin board

STITCHES: Long Stitch
Diagonal Mosaic
Basketweave (in a color slightly darker than the pots)
Needleweaving
Binding Stitch
Hungarian

CANVAS: Interlock Mono 14, 12" × 18" (3" margins included) and approximately 2½" × 2½" for each of four flowers; Plastic, 10. 1½" × 4½" for both flower pots

YARN: Tapestry or Persian

NEEDLE: Size 20

SIZE OF FINISHED PROJECT: 6" × 12"

THE METHODS OF THREE-DIMENSIONAL NEEDLEPOINT

Work the background in Long Stitch. You *must* stitch on a frame. Be sure to strip the yarn (page 19). Stitch the flowers and the pots.

Cut out the flower petals so that there is about ⅛" of blank canvas around the stitching (Figure 6-2c). Glue a big fuzzy pipe cleaner on the ⅛" edge of blank canvas on each petal. Allow the tab to extend below the pipe cleaner for about ¼". Allow the glue to dry thoroughly. Hint: Buy the pipe cleaners first; then select the yarn colors. It's much easier to match colors that way. Glue a lining fabric to the back of each petal.

Cut out the pots (Figure 6-2d) so that there is 1 mesh all the way around the pot. See also Figure 5-2d. Work the Binding Stitch across the top of the pot. Attach the pots to the space indicated on the background along the sides and bottom with a Whipstitch. They will bow out slightly, giving a three-dimensional look.

Fold a green pipe cleaner as shown in Figure 6-2c to make a leaf. Fill the form with Needleweaving. Stick the leaves down into the flower pots. Secure them to the background canvas with sewing thread.

Lay the tabs of five flower petals as shown in Figure 6-2f overlapping the petals. Stitch through all five thicknesses of canvas with sewing thread. Take several random stitches to hold the petals together. With the same thread, sew the flowers to the background where you would like them to be.

Wind a brown fuzzy pipe cleaner into a coil. It should be big enough to cover the tabs of blank canvas in the centers of the flowers. Glue it in place, and allow it to dry *completely*.

Staple the needlepoint to a piece of ¼" plywood (see framing on page 247). Insert it into a bulletin board like the one pictured here. Have someone who's handy with a saw make one for you—or order it from the source listed on page 261.

FIG. 6-2a *Bulletin Board.*

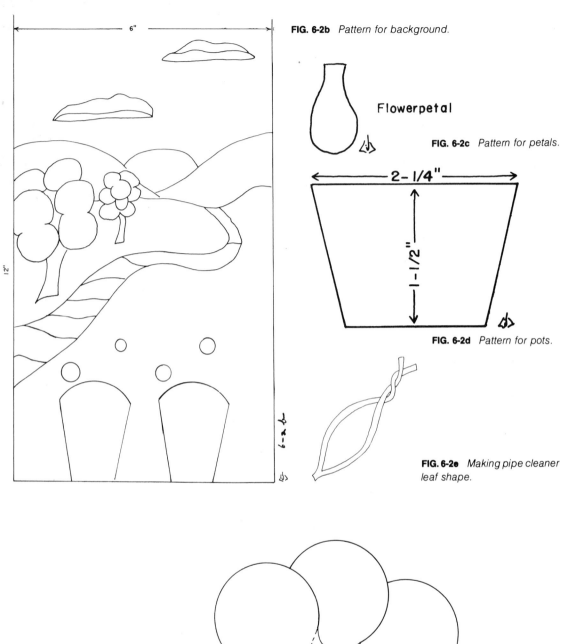

6"

12"

6-2-f

FIG. 6-2b *Pattern for background.*

Flowerpetal

FIG. 6-2c *Pattern for petals.*

2-1/4"

1-1/2"

FIG. 6-2d *Pattern for pots.*

FIG. 6-2e *Making pipe cleaner leaf shape.*

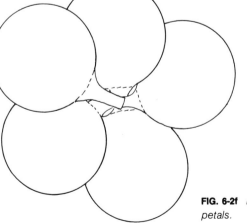

FIG. 6-2f *Forming flower from petals.*

STITCHES: Basketweave (I used Brick and it doesn't look so nice as one stitched in Basketweave, so I really can't recommend Brick.)

CANVAS: Interlock Mono 14: background—12½″ × 17″ (3″ margins included); rainbows—approximately 16″ × 22″ (all necessary margins included). Use scraps if you can; however, straight grain must be followed as marked in Figure 6-3c–g.

YARN: Persian—Paternayan colors given on page 93 for Figure 6-3c–f (numbers in diagram correspond with color numbers).

NEEDLE: Size 20

SIZE OF FINISHED PROJECT: 6½″ × 11″ × 2½″

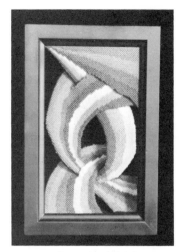

FIG. 6-3a *Intertwined Rainbows.*

Stitch all pieces as shown in Figure 6-3c–f. Keep the curves as smooth as you can. Block as described on page 241.

The photo series beginning with Figure 6-3h shows you how to finish and assemble the pieces into a finished product. You will need a working or assembly frame to do this. Have it made so that the *inside* measurement is *exactly* 6½″ × 11″. It should be made of ½″ stock. It needs to be 1⅝″ deep. Two slashes should be cut in the upper right and lower right corners. See Figure 6-3g for the measurements. Paint the inside of this frame black.

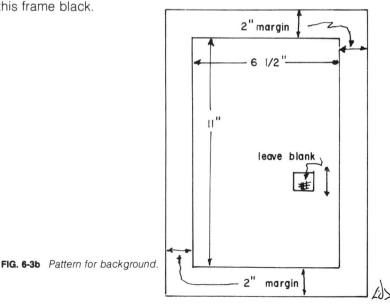

2″ margin

6 1/2″

11″

leave blank

FIG. 6-3b *Pattern for background.*

2″ margin

FIG. 6-3c *Pattern for rainbow A.*

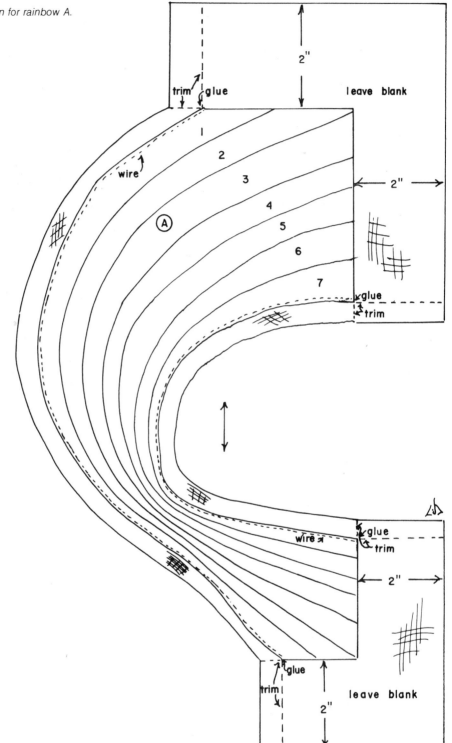

THE METHODS OF THREE-DIMENSIONAL NEEDLEPOINT

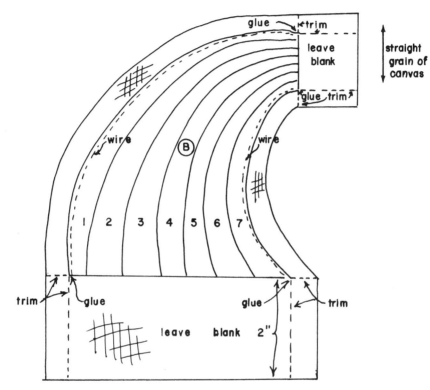

FIG. 6-3d *Pattern for rainbow B.*

PATERNAYAN COLOR NUMBERS

1. 642	5. 456
2. 733	6. 960
3. 310	7. 200
4. 508	

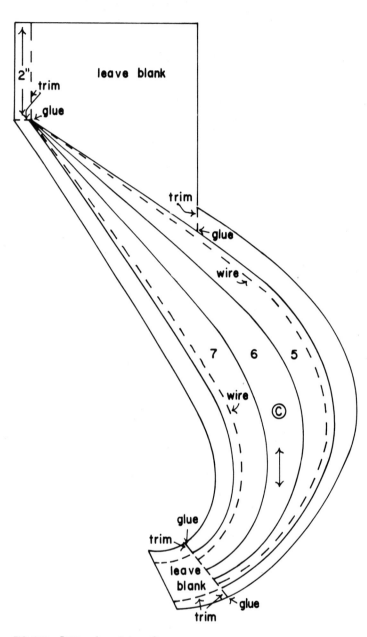

FIG. 6-3e *Pattern for rainbow C.*

THE METHODS OF THREE-DIMENSIONAL NEEDLEPOINT

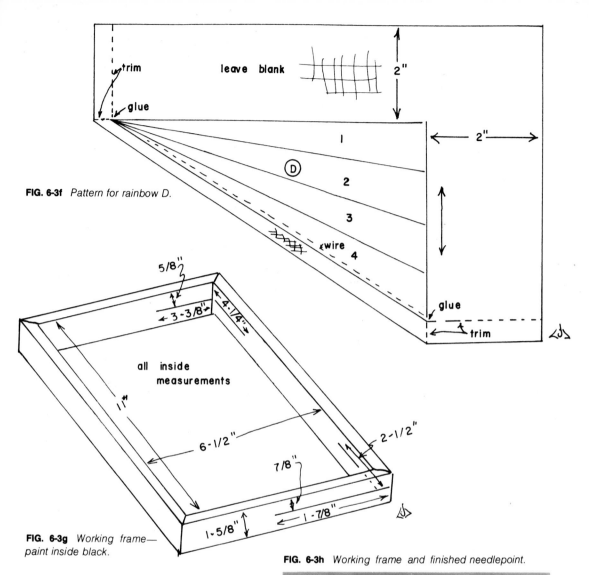

leave blank

2"

trim

glue

2"

I

D

2

3

wire

4

glue

trim

J

FIG. 6-3f *Pattern for rainbow D.*

5/8"

3 - 3/8"

4-1/4"

all inside
measurements

1"

6-1/2"

2-1/2"

7/8"

1-5/8"

1-7/8"

J

FIG. 6-3g *Working frame—
paint inside black.*

FIG. 6-3h *Working frame and finished needlepoint.*

6½" X 11"

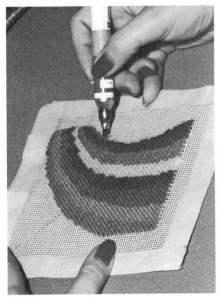

FIG. 6-3i *Paint canvas edges around stitching with same color as yarn.*

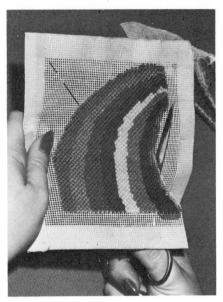

FIG. 6-3j *Cut the canvas as shown in Figures 6-3c–f.*

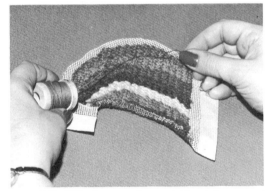

FIG. 6-3k *Sew medium-weight, cloth-covered florists' wire to the edges of the stitching (Figures 6-3c–f).*

FIG. 6-3l *I have not painted the margins of canvas, so you can see them better. Moisten the margin of blank canvas with a little water on your fingertip.*

FIG. 6-3m *Turn the hem and whipstitch with sewing thread the same color as the yarn. Your stitches should not show on the right side of the needlepoint. Catch the wire.*

FIG. 6-3n *Moisten only a small section at one time.*

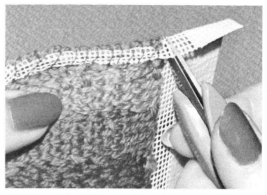

FIG. 6-3o *Clip at the end of the needlepoint stitches.*

FIG. 6-3p *Trim away the excess canvas. Put a dot of glue where the canvas is cut to the stitches.*

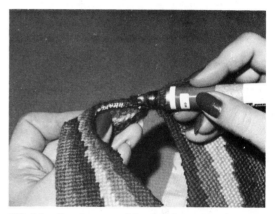

FIG. 6-3q *Touch up any bits of white canvas that show.*

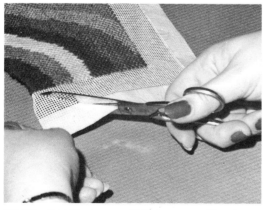

FIG. 6-3r *Trim the corners of blank canvas of the pieces that will go through the slots in the frame. The canvas goes through the slots easier this way.*

FIG. 6-3s *Put a dot of glue where the slash meets the stitches.*

Detached canvas

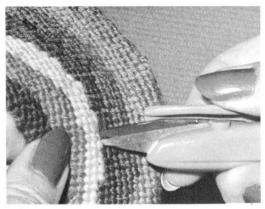

FIG. 6-3t Carefully cut the canvas between the stitches on the lines indicated in Figures 6-3c and d. (Really! Your stitching will not fall apart!!)

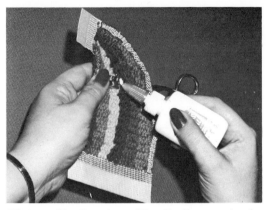

FIG. 6-3u Glue the edges of the slits. Keep moving the canvas so it doesn't glue back together. Allow it to dry thoroughly before you continue to the next steps using these pieces.

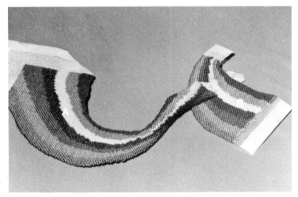

FIG. 6-3v Insert piece A through piece B. Roll the smaller tab on piece A so it will go through the slot on piece B.

FIG. 6-3w Slide piece A to the narrow neck. The two pieces should lie flat and smoothly now. If they don't, your slot may not be big enough.

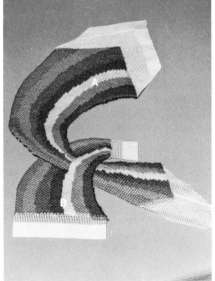

FIG. 6-3x Slip the small tab on piece C through the slot in piece A. You'll need to lift up piece B to get at it. (When I stitched mine, pieces C and D were combined. It works better to separate them—so I did for you. That's why you see piece D attached to piece C now. Don't do yours yet.)

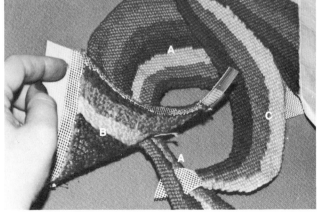

FIG. 6-3y *Stitch the tab of piece C to the underside of piece A.*

FIG. 6-3z *Trim the excess canvas of the tab of piece C. It should not show from the right side.*

FIG. 6-3aa *The underside of piece A should look like this now.*

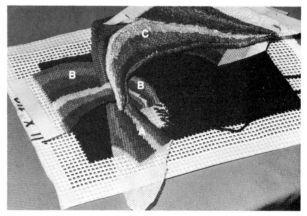

FIG. 6-3bb *Now place the tab of piece B over the blank square of canvas on the large rectangular piece you stitched in black. The blank square should be closest to the lower right-hand corner.*

FIG. 6-3cc *Paint the tab and the blank square black. I left mine till now so you could see it. Stitch through both thicknesses of canvas as if they were one. (I did not use canvases of the same size, so it was harder to do. Yours will be easier to stitch.)*

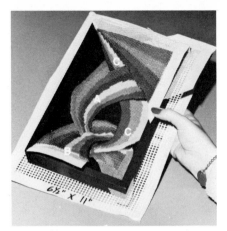

FIG. 6-3dd *Put piece C under piece A. Roll the tab, and insert it through the slot in piece A. It should lie reasonably flat. Lay the working frame on top of the needlepoint. The larger slot should be in the upper right corner. The smaller slot should be in the lower right corner. Put the smaller tab on piece A through the smaller slot.*

FIG. 6-3ee *Insert the larger tab of piece A through the larger slot. (Your D piece is still not on.)*

FIG. 6-3ff *Paint the canvas if any white shows after you've pulled the tab through the slot.*

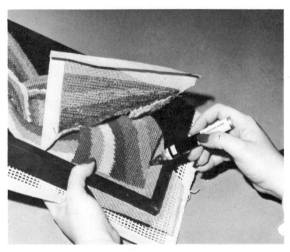

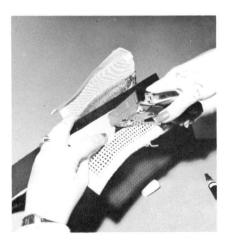

FIG. 6-3gg *Staple piece A's tabs to the frame.*

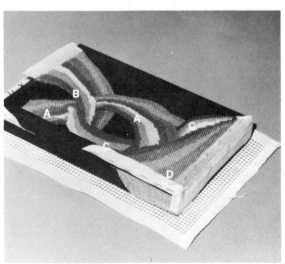

FIG. 6-3hh *Now lay piece D across the top, and staple it to the frame. Hand tack or glue it to piece C, so that the white canvas tab of piece C does not show.*

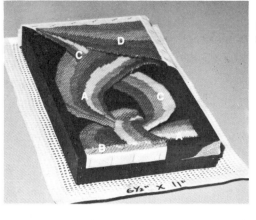

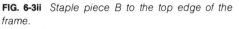

FIG. 6-3ii *Staple piece B to the top edge of the frame.*

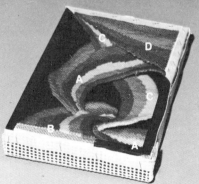

FIG. 6-3jj *Staple the bottom rectangular piece to the outside of the working frame. Now all you need is a decorative frame. I'm sure this looks like an awful mess, but if you take it step by step, you'll find it's not nearly as difficult as it seems. It's really very well organized.*

When the whole piece is finally put together, you will need a decorative frame to cover your working frame (page 253).

House

STITCHES:
1. Basketweave
2. Continental
3. Framed Cashmere
4. Framed Scotch
5. Horizontal Brick
6. Straight Stitch
7. Split Gobelin
8. Shingle Stitch
9. Cut Turkey Work
10. Leaf #1
    Looped Turkey Work (evergreen trees)
    Binding Stitch

FIG. 6-4a *House.*

CANVAS: Interlock Mono 10, 17" × 30" (3" margins included); Plastic 10, 8" × 11" (no margins needed) or scraps

YARN: Tapestry or Persian; pearl cotton for window and grill

NEEDLE: Size 18 or 20

SIZE OF FINISHED PROJECT: 8" × 24" × 3"

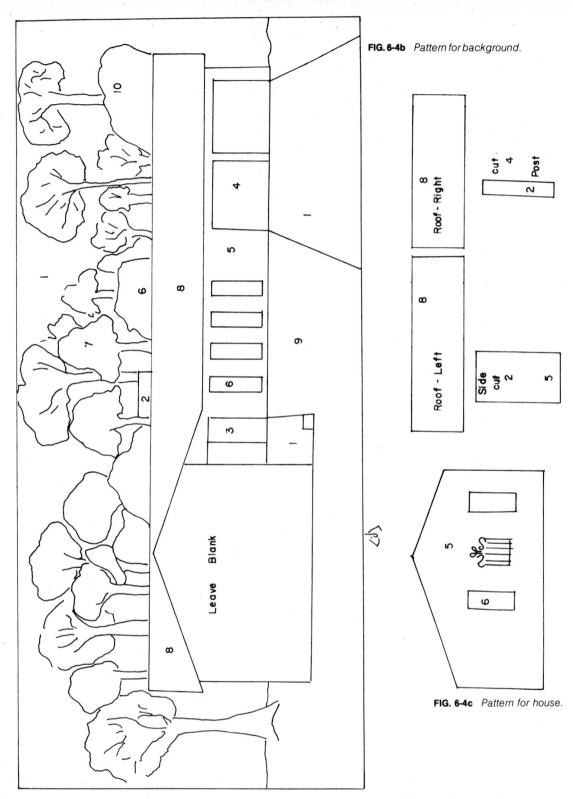

FIG. 6-4b *Pattern for background.*

Roof - Right 8

cut
4
Post
2

Roof - Left 8

Side
cut
2
5

Leave Blank

FIG. 6-4c *Pattern for house.*

FIG. 6-4d *Real house.*   **FIG. 6-4e** *Close-up of trees.*

I realize that you all don't have houses that look like Mickey's! However, if I show you the techniques that she used, you can probably apply most of them to recreating your house.

First, you'll need to take pictures of your house. Blow a whole roll of black-and-white film, and take pictures from *all* angles—especially if your house is more than one rectangle. These will help you decide on the angle to stitch. They will also help you to study your house and stitch it correctly. If you have a blueprint, it will give you a good pattern to use.

Stitch the background canvas first. Leave blank the place where the three-dimensional part of the L-shaped house will be attached. Work the sky right up to the tree trunks—with no spaces left for the pine needles or leaves. Use one ply of Persian yarn to stitch the pine needles. This will give a lacy look to them. Work them right over the Basketweave sky. This is a lot easier than trying to fit Basketweave in between pine needles—or other kinds of tree leaves. Use the chapter on Leaf Stitches as a basis for stitching the leaves—then do your own thing (see Figure 6-4e).

Block (page 241). While the piece is still on the blocking board, mow the grass! (Don't trim the Turkey Work before this. It's OK to cut the loops, but don't even it out.) Use scissors or—better yet—a pair of barber's clippers to mow the grass. Scissors for Bunka embroidery are a good substitute.

Next, stitch the pieces of plastic canvas. Remember the underside of the roof is usually painted the same color as the house's trim. Sew the house together with an Overcast

Detached canvas

Stitch or the Binding Stitch. Attach the house to the underside of the roof. Put the post together with an Overcast Stitch. Sew it to the underside of the roof.

Put the pieces of the roof together (wrong sides together) with the Binding Stitch. Using an Overcast or Whipstitch, attach the house to the background canvas along the sides and along the roof—not at the bottom yet.

You will need an assembly or working frame to put the needlepoint into. See Figure 6-4f for the size of this frame.

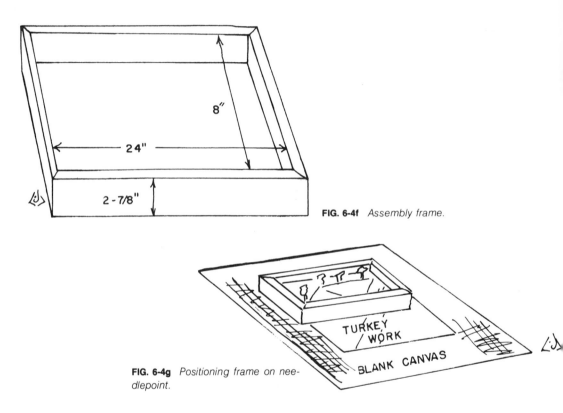

FIG. 6-4f *Assembly frame.*

FIG. 6-4g *Positioning frame on needlepoint.*

Paint the two short sides and one long side blue (sky) on the inside.

Now put the needlepoint onto the working frame. Using a staple gun, staple the needlepoint to the frame (Figure 6-4g). Lay the needlepoint down on a table. Put the frame on top of it, so that the frame sits on blank canvas at the top and on both sides. The inside of the bottom edge of the frame should be on the horizon line, and the bottom of the frame will sit on the grass. Turn the whole thing over, and staple the frame to the blank canvas only. That means the bottom will not be stapled yet (Figure 6-4h).

THE METHODS OF THREE-DIMENSIONAL NEEDLEPOINT

Slash the canvas to the stitching on the heavy black lines in Figure 6-4h. Put a dot of glue where the cut meets the stitches. Let it dry.

Push the free-hanging flap of canvas through to the inside of the frame. The grass will now lie flat against the inside of the bottom of the frame. Pull the canvas (grass) slightly forward. Staple the horizon line to the inside of the bottom of the frame. It will have to slant inward about ⅛", but it won't be noticeable. Push the house back with the staple gun to get in there to staple. It shouldn't hurt the house. The Turkey Work will hide the staples.

Now is the time to sew the bottom of the house to the canvas. Use an Overcast Stitch. It will be awkward, but it can be done. Don't worry if your stitches aren't the neatest—the Turkey Work will hide most of them.

Make the shrubs from scraps of Interlock Mono canvas. Cut different-sized triangles and circles—according to the size of the space to be filled. Stitch them in Looped Turkey Work and Leaf Stitches. Form the triangles into cones, and whip the seams with one ply of green Persian yarn. Work a

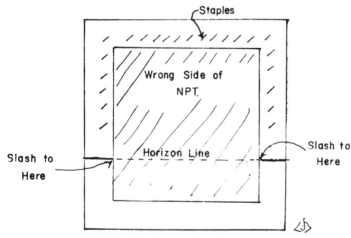

FIG. 6-4h *Stapling needlepoint to frame.*

FIG. 6-4i *Close-up of evergreen tree.*

running stitch around the bottom of each tree. Pull the running thread slightly to give the tree some shape and to tuck in the raw edges of the canvas. Attach it to the grass with an Overcast Stitch.

Work the circles the same way—only there's no seam to stitch—and pull the drawstring tightly to make a round bush. Use that same thread to sew it to the grass.

Finally, staple the front part of the grass to the working frame. Staple the margins of blank canvas to the frame. All the needlepoint needs now is a decorative frame (page 253).

THE METHODS OF THREE-DIMENSIONAL NEEDLEPOINT

PLATE 1 Christmas Wreath, designed by Mary Savage and the author, stitched by Mary Savage.

PLATE 2
Four Seasons Bell Pull,
designed and stitched
by Nyla Christensen.

PLATE 3
Christmas Wreath Ornament,
designed and stitched
by the author.

PLATE 5
(opposite page) Apple Tree Mirror,
designed by Ed Sibbett, Jr., and stitched by the author.

PLATE 4   Christmas Mobile, designed and stitched by Betty Powers.

PLATE 6 Stacked Cubes, designed and stitched by
Wayne Stephens.

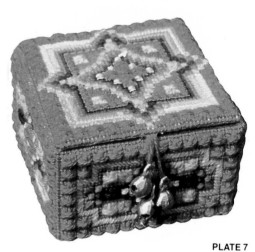

PLATE 7
Jody's Needlepoint Box,
designed and stitched by Jody House.

PLATE 9 (opposite page)
Intertwined Rainbows, designed
and stitched by the author.

PLATE 8 (left) Three-Dimensional Cube,
designed and stitched by Barbara Johnston,
background stitched by Diana Smith.

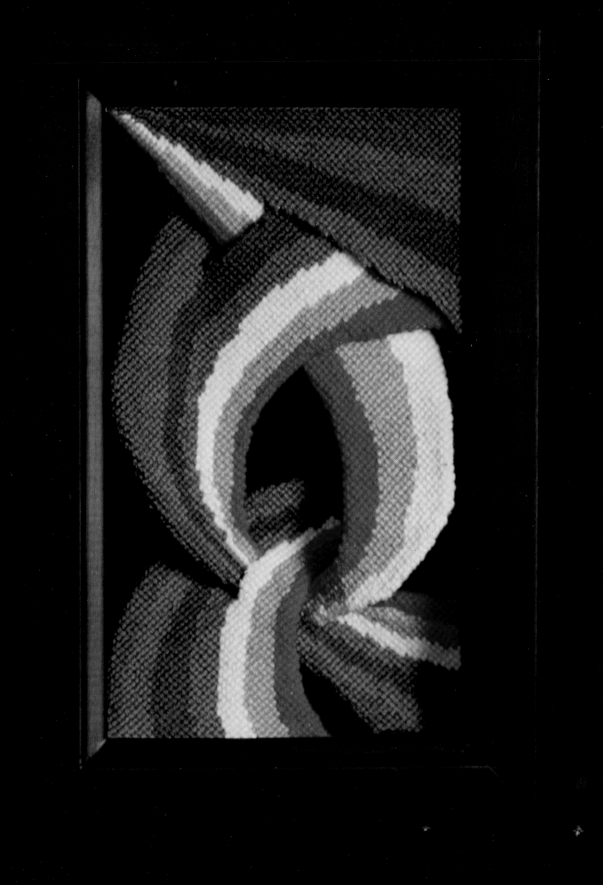

PLATE 10 Scissors Case, designed and stitched by Nyla Christensen.

PLATE 11 Black-Eyed Susan Purse, designed by Nina West, stitched by the author.

PLATE 12A Triangle, designed and stitched by Barbara Johnston.

PLATE 12B Close-up of Triangle.

PLATE 13 Ballet Slippers, designed by Jackie Beaty and the author, stitched by Jackie Beaty. Lettering designed by Doris Drake.

PLATE 14 Bulletin Board, designed by Jackie Beaty and the author, stitched by Jackie Beaty.

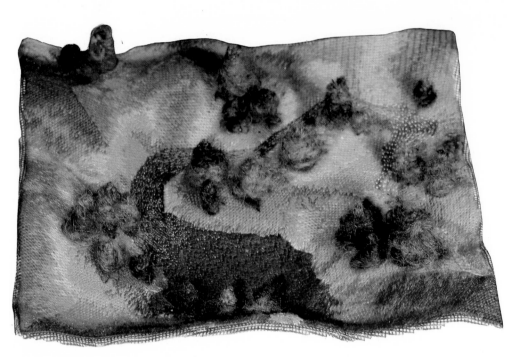

PLATE 15 Close-up of Landscape Table Top.

PLATE 16 Landscape Table Top, designed and stitched by the author.

PLATE 17 (left)
Black Cat, designed and stitched by the author.

PLATE 18 (below)
Airplane, designed by Carole Key and the author,
stitched by Carole Key, and assembled by the author.

PLATE 19 (left) Waste Knot, Want Knot, designed and stitched by Pat Means.

PLATE 20 (below) Basket of Flowers, designed and stitched by the author.

PLATE 21 Northwest Autumn, designed and stitched by Pat Means.

PLATE 22
Mother and Child,
designed by Cynthia M. Pendleton,
stitched by Jackie Beaty

PLATE 23
Needlepoint Shop,
designed and stitched
by Lois Ann Necaise.

PLATE 24 Golf Cart, designed and stitched by Diana Smith.

PLATE 25 House, designed by Mickey McKitrick and the author, stitched by Mickey McKitrick.

PLATE 26 Car, designed and stitched by the author.

PLATE 27 (opposite page)
Apple, designed by the author, stitched by Linda Kilgore.

PLATE 28 Farm, designed and stitched by Nyla Christensen.

Chapter 7

Appliqué

Appliqué of one canvas to another allows versatility in design. As in the Landscape, an optical illusion can be created. The lake seems farther away, because the stitches are smaller than those around it. The viewer of the car is more aware of the car's shape when the appliqué is stuffed. A smaller canvas allows more detail, as in the car's grillwork. The faces of the Mother and Child are more delicate when stitched on a smaller canvas. The shading of the Apple is more easily accomplished on a smaller canvas. Also, the Apple seems more real with a roundness (given by stuffing the appliqué).

In this book I discuss two ways to appliqué one canvas onto another. The Landscape, Car, and Mother and Child make use of one type, and the Apple makes use of another.

Landscape table top

STITCHES: 1. Interlocking Gobelin
               2. Bargello (see Figure 7-1d)
               3. Chain
                   Looped Turkey Work (trees)
                   Buttonhole (tree trunks)

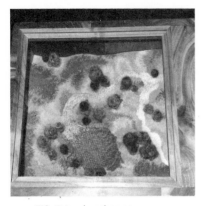

FIG. 7-1a *Landscape.*

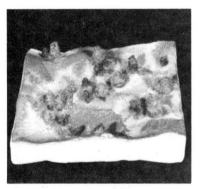

FIG. 7-1b *Close-up of Landscape.*

FIG. 7-1c *View of whole table.*

CANVAS: Interlock Mono 10, 24″ × 24″ (approximately 3″ margins included); lake—Nylon 20, 6″ × 6″.

YARN: Persian, #5 pearl cotton and/or rayon floss (water), variegated green mohair (trees)

NEEDLE: Sizes 20 and 22

SIZE OF FINISHED PROJECT: 13″ × 13″ × 2″

The stitched needlepoint is attached to a plaster of Paris mold. The photo series in Figure 7-1g–s shows how to make the mold and ready your canvas for stitching.

While your canvas is drying, stitch the lake. Block (page 241). Trim the canvas to within ½″ of the stitching. Melt the edges of the nylon canvas with a match. It will not ravel now. Then baste the lake to the area for the lake on the big piece of canvas.

Stitch all but the lake and stream in Interlocking Gobelin. This stitch distorts the canvas horribly—and for once that's *good!* Mark the tops of the hills with a bit of yarn. Slant the stitch, and turn the canvas so that the crest of the hill is always at the top of the area you're working on. Figure 7-1b shows how to turn the stitch. Some of your stitches will look awful until you get the hang of it. Cover them with trees later on, and no one will ever know but you and me! (And I won't tell!)

I used three greens and three golds to stitch the ground. On Mono 10 canvas, three ply of Persian is used. Mark off your canvas into areas for color changes. Letter each of the yarns from A to F. Refer to the following charts to *guide* you in shading.

FIG. 7-1d *Bargello for lake.*

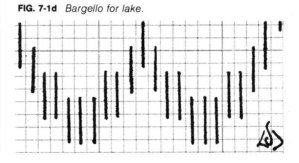

3-PLY YARN	4-PLY YARN
Area	Area

Area	3-PLY YARN	Area	4-PLY YARN
1	AAA	1	AAAA
2	AAB	2	AAAB
3	ABB	3	AABB
4	BBB	4	ABBB
5	BBC	5	BBBB
6	BCC	6	BBBC
7	CCC	7	BBCC
8	CCD	8	BCCC
9	CDD	9	CCCC
10	DDD	10	CCCD
11	DDE	11	CCDD
12	DEE	12	CDDD
13	EEE	13	DDDD
		14	DDDE
		15	DDEE
		16	DEEE
		17	EEEE

This is not a shading project that must be exact. One hill may be a shading process from colors A and B to E and F. Another run of colors may be A, B, C, F; another, B, D, F; whatever grabs you at the moment.

When you get to the margin of the nylon canvas that has been appliquéd onto the big canvas, stitch through both thicknesses of canvas as if they were one. It's easier to start stitching at the water's edge and work out through the margin of blank canvas. Follow the mesh of the bigger canvas to maintain the stitch size. If you're having trouble seeing the larger canvas's mesh, hold it up to the light to see where to put your needle. Because the nylon canvas is so thin, no ridge will show. If bits of mesh poke between stitches, just cut them off—they're not going anywhere.

Appliqué always does best on a frame. Try it.

Stitch the water in the Chain Stitch. I used six shades of blue and shaded them according to the chart. Gradually disperse the ends of the Chain Stitch in the Bargello of the lake. I had to mix rayon floss and pearl cotton to get the six colors I needed. It worked. But since pearl cotton does not separate, I merely wrapped varying amounts of rayon floss around the pearl cotton. So some strands were thicker than others. It doesn't show, now that it's finished.

FIG. 7-1e *Have a wooden box built that will serve as a container for clay and plaster. The sides and bottom should come apart. Mine was 6" deep, but 3½" or 4" would have been enough. It is 13" x 13". Using artist's clay, mold a landscape of hills, valleys, a stream, and a lake. Do not allow the clay to dry.*

Follow Figures 2-21g–kk for the rest of the instructions for this project. I had a table built around the needlepoint. See page 262 for information on ordering a table to go with your needlepoint.

FIG. 7-1f *Be sure the clay goes to the sides of the box. Use a knife to clean up the edge.*

FIG. 7-1g *Mix plaster of Paris according to the directions on the package. Pour it over the clay. It should be about 1" deep at the highest point of the clay.*

FIG. 7-1h *Lay a piece of cheesecloth over the plaster to strengthen it.*

FIG. 7-1i *When the plaster has dried, take the sides apart, and lift out the plaster. This is the mold.*

FIG. 7-1j *Put the box back together. Put the plaster mold inside. Fill the edges and corners with clay if necessary.*

FIG. 7-1k *Cover the surface of the plaster generously with tincture of green soap (from a drugstore). This keeps the next layer of plaster from sticking to the plaster mold.*

FIG. 7-1l *Pour plaster in as you did before. Put in another piece of cheesecloth.*

FIG. 7-1m *Spread the plaster evenly with a piece of cardboard.*

FIG. 7-1n *When the plaster has dried, remove it from the box. You now have a plaster replica of your clay.*

Appliqué

FIG. 7-1o *In case you don't have a basement or garage to pour plaster in—or if you have kids who want to help—a papier-mâché form can be made. Cover the clay with a plastic bag. Dip strips of newspaper in white glue (or PVA from art supply stores) that has been thinned with a little water. Allow the glue to dry between layers of newspaper. When the form is thick enough and stiff enough to stand alone, remove the clay. Work the papier-mâché from the inside now. This takes lots of man-hours.*

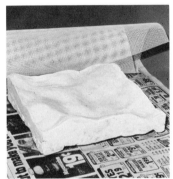

FIG. 7-1p *Sand the plaster to smooth very rough edges.*

FIG. 7-1q *Lay a piece of damp canvas over the plaster mold. There should be enough margins to turn to the underside of the plaster.*

FIG. 7-1r *Tuck the canvas under. Put a wet dishcloth over the canvas. Weight it down in the valleys with anything that will fit and that is heavy enough to do the job. Be sure everything is rust- and stainproof. Allow the canvas to dry.*

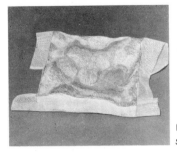

FIG. 7-1s *Paint the canvas while it is still on the mold.*

FIG. 7-1t *Stitch with the Interlocking Gobelin Stitch. Turn as shown here to force the distortion to work for you.*

FIG. 7-1u *The canvas will rise to a peak—which is useful in creating hilltops.*

FIG. 7-1v *Shade with scattered stitches and according to the chart on page 108.*

Appliqué

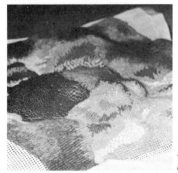

FIG. 7-1w *The finished canvas will be filled with wonderful lumps and bumps!*

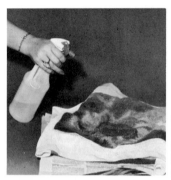

FIG. 7-1x *Moisten the yarn well with a spray of water. Apply a coat of white glue to the plaster. Stretch it over the plaster form. Lace it on securely. Line up the edge of the stitching with the edge of the form. Don't worry about getting the canvas to sink into the depressions yet. Cover the needlepoint with a large piece of clean white paper or fabric. Then spread a large piece of plastic over that.*

FIG. 7-1y *Fill the depressions with kitty litter (yes—you read it right!) or sand. Pour water over it all to make it heavy. It will force the canvas down. Leave it overnight, and hope the cat doesn't get any ideas! Remove the kitty litter, plastic bag, and paper. Allow the needlepoint to dry another couple of days. When it is thoroughly dry, the trees can be put on.*

FIG. 7-1z *Paint round toothpicks with a marker.*

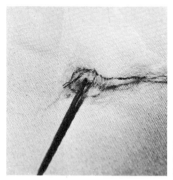

FIG. 7-1aa *Using variegated mo-hair, tie a knot around one end of the toothpick.*

FIG. 7-1bb *Work the Chain Stitch down the toothpick, catching the tail as you go. If you knit, you may find it easier to cast the stitches on.*

FIG. 7-1cc *Work Looped Turkey Work on Chain Stitches. Go around and around in a spiral—up the toothpick. Make the loops big at the bottom, and reduce their size as you go up.*

FIG. 7-1dd *Vary the length of the stitches put on the toothpick, and vary the size of the loops. The first loops you make will be the base of the tree and thus the biggest on each tree.*

Appliqué

FIG. 7-1ee *Push the tree to the bottom of the toothpick.*

FIG. 7-1ff *Break off the toothpick at the top of the tree.*

FIG. 7-1gg *The top of the tree will look like this.*

FIG. 7-1hh *Push the tree up the toothpick until the toothpick disappears.*

THE METHODS OF THREE-DIMENSIONAL NEEDLEPOINT

FIG. 7-1ii *There will then be just enough toothpick at the base of the tree to put it onto the needlepoint.*

FIG. 7-1jj *Drill holes (⁵/₆₄″) in the plaster—right through the needlepoint—for the trees. Dip the toothpicks in white glue, and push them into the holes.*

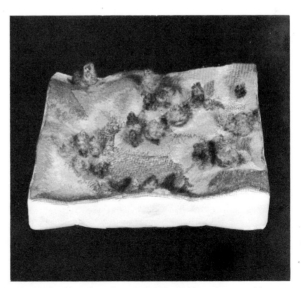

FIG. 7-1kk *Now the piece is ready to insert into a table.*

Car

STITCHES: 1. Hungarian
                2. Upright Cross
                3. Shisha
                4. Chain
                5. Cashmere
                6. Continental
                7. Oriental
                8. Lazy Kalem

CANVAS: Interlock Mono 10, 14″ × 24″ (3″ margins included); Nylon 20, 4″ × 14″ (½″ margin included)

YARN: Tapestry or Persian; windshield and car body, pearl cotton; silver metallic, grill and chrome; embroidery floss, tires and windshield wipers

NEEDLE: Sizes 20 and 22

SIZE OF FINISHED PROJECT: 8″ × 18″

Stitch the body of the car first. Paint the canvas in the grill area a dark grey. Most of it will show. Work the Chain Stitch around the top of the grill and down the grill as shown in Figure 7-2c. Lay diagonal threads across the grill area at more even intervals than I did. Secure the junction with an Upright Cross Stitch. Be careful how you drag the yarn across the back of the canvas, for it will show on the front if it does not follow the pattern. Attach the headlights with the Shisha Stitch. See page 261 for a mail-order source.

    Block (page 241). Trim the canvas, and melt the edges as described for the Landscape Table Top on page 108.

    Securely baste the nylon canvas to the background. It's a hair bigger, so ease it in if you have to.

FIG. 7-2a *Car.*

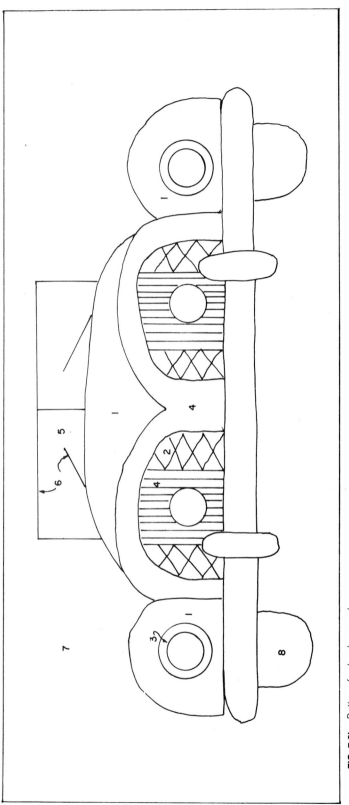

FIG. 7-2b *Pattern for background.*

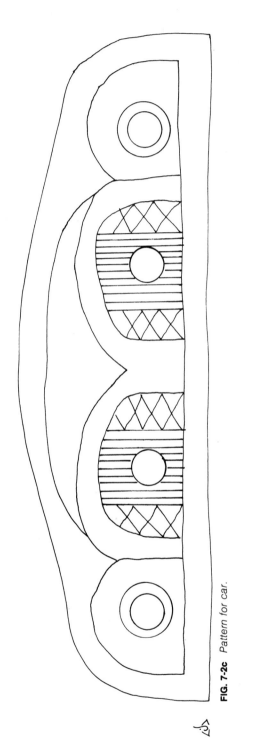

FIG. 7-2c *Pattern for car.*

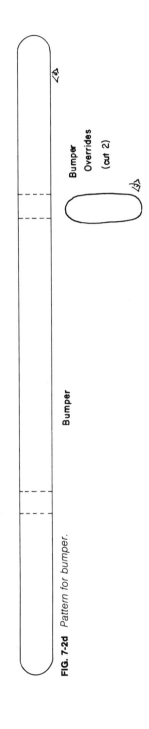

Bumper

Bumper Overrides (cut 2)

FIG. 7-2d *Pattern for bumper.*

THE METHODS OF THREE-DIMENSIONAL NEEDLEPOINT

Stitch the background and the windshield through both thicknesses of canvas as described for the Landscape Table Top on page 109. Stuff from the bottom edge with polyester fiber. Baste the bottom edge of canvas back in place—over the blank bumper.

Block (page 241).

Cut a piece of silver kid in the shape of the bumper. Split the silver metallic you used for the chrome. With tiny stitches of silver thread on a fine needle, sew the kid in place. Stuff with polyester fiber before you stitch an area closed.

Staple the finished needlepoint to a piece of ¼" plywood, and use as a picture or a box top. The elegant box may be ordered from the address on page 262.

FIG. 7-2e *Close-up.*

Mother and child

STITCHES: 1. Brick
2. Basketweave
3. Continental
4. Upright Cross
5. Bullion Knots
6. Couching

CANVAS: Mono (Regular or Interlock) 14, 15½" × 18½" (3" margins included); Nylon 20, approximately 5" × 6" (for mother's face and hands and baby's face)

YARN: Persian, linen (faces and hands), #5 pearl cotton (lips)

NEEDLE: Sizes 20 and 22

SIZE OF FINISHED PROJECT: 9½" × 12½"

FIG. 7-3a *Mother and Child.*

Appliqué of canvas and fabric was combined here to create a soft, feminine look. First stitch the two faces and Mama's hand on the nylon canvas. Block (page 241). Cut them out, melt edges, appliqué, and stuff, using the same techniques as you did for the Landscape Table Top (pages 108–9) and the Car (pages 118–21). The only exception is—do not stitch Mama's face to the canvas at the hairline. Sew it to a piece of lightweight fabric the same color and shape as her hair. See Figure 7-3n. Sew it down all around the outside edges after you've stuffed Mama's face and hair. Use tiny stitches of sewing thread.

FIG. 7-3b *Pattern of Mother and Child.*

Stitch the background and baby's blanket. See page 109 for instructions on stitching through nylon canvas. Block (page 241). Use yarn for Mama's hair. Couch it down by securing the yarn with sewing thread, piercing only the fabric and one ply of the 3- (or 4-) ply yarn.

Cut the yoke and sleeve patterns out of fabric. A polyester and cotton pink fabric was used here for an underlining. (The canvas shows through if you don't use an underlining.) Cut it to size with no seam allowances. Baste it in place, but

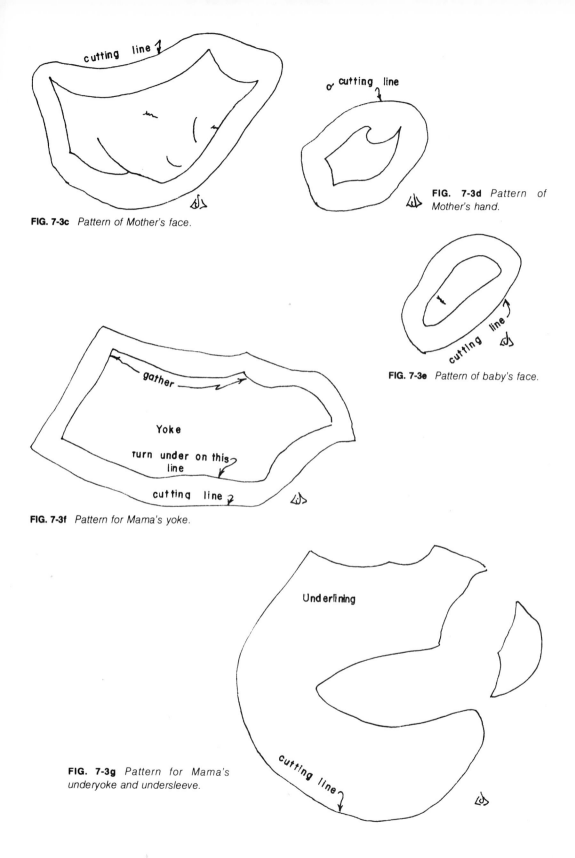

FIG. 7-3c *Pattern of Mother's face.*

FIG. 7-3d *Pattern of Mother's hand.*

FIG. 7-3e *Pattern of baby's face.*

FIG. 7-3f *Pattern for Mama's yoke.*

FIG. 7-3g *Pattern for Mama's underyoke and undersleeve.*

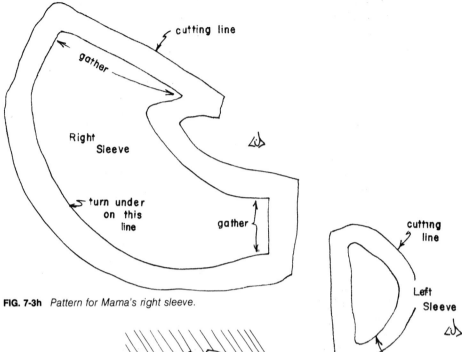

FIG. 7-3h *Pattern for Mama's right sleeve.*

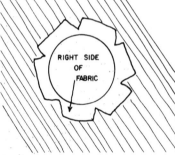

FIG. 7-3j *Turning edge on fabric.*

FIG. 7-3I *Pattern for Mama's left sleeve.*

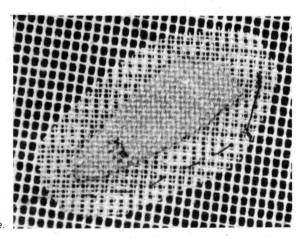

FIG. 7-3k *Close-up of baby's face.*

THE METHODS OF THREE-DIMENSIONAL NEEDLEPOINT

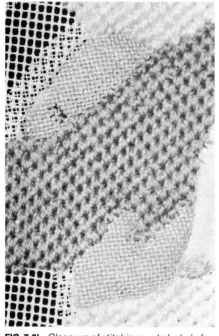

FIG. 7-3l *Close-up of stitching up to baby's face and Mama's hand.*

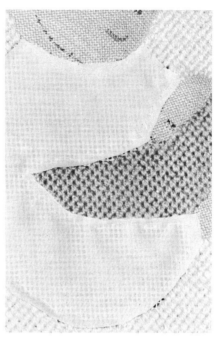

FIG. 7-3m *Hand tack underlining in place.*

FIG. 7-3n *Tack fabric in place for hair. Stuff lightly with polyester fiber.*

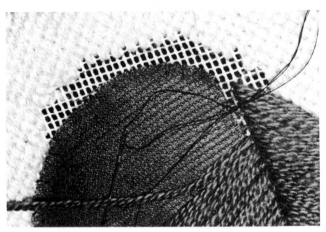

FIG. 7-3o *Couch yarn (for hair) in place over fabric.*

leave the edges free, so the seam allowances of the outer fabric can be tucked under the underlining. This is not necessary at the neck and the wrist. Turn under the raw edges of the yoke at the neck, the sleeve at the wrist, and the top of the sleeve. Turn these edges under ¼", and stitch on the sewing machine with a long stitch. Pull this thread, and gather the fabric so that it is the proper size to fit the space allotted. This turns the raw edge under and gathers in the same operation. Baste these gathered edges in place. Slip the bottom edge of the yoke under the top edge of the sleeve before you baste it in place. Next turn the rest of the raw edges under the underlining. Sew with the Blind Stitch (page 255). Tack a tiny lace and pearl trim onto the gathered seams.

Note: Because Jackie and I both thought that Mama's gathers could have come out better, the pattern was revised. I'm giving the new one to you. Isn't hindsight wonderful?

Make *very loose* Bullion Knots for Mama's topknot: Couch both Mama's and baby's curls in place. If baby is a girl, tie a tiny bow from the pearl cotton that you used for the lips. Use a long strand that you can handle easily; then cut off the excess.

Do not dampen after the fabric has been added to the canvas. So don't block again.

Stretch it over a 13" × 16" piece of ¼" plywood as described on page 251. Cut a piece of Masonite 13" × 16" to put the velvet on (for a mat). Spread fabric glue on the Masonite with an old brush. Lay the velvet smoothly over the glued surface. Next, cut the hole out of the center, leaving a 1" margin. Slash the fabric, and bring it to the wrong side. Glue the pieces in place. See Figure 7-3j. If the fabric does not turn easily, DO NOT make slashes deeper. SLASH MORE OFTEN.

Frame according to the directions on page 247.

STITCHES: 1. Reversed Scotch
2. Roumanian Leaf
3. Raised Buttonhole on Raised Band
Byzantine (background)

CANVAS: Background—Mono (Regular or Interlock) 10, 11″ × 11″ (3″ margins included); apple—Regular Mono 14, 10″ × 10″ (3″ margins included); leaf—Interlock Mono 14, 1½″ × 2½″ (¼″ margin included)

FIG. 7-4a *Apple.*

YARN: Tapestry or Persian (for shading—five colors for the apple)

NEEDLE: Size 20

SIZE OF FINISHED PROJECT: 5″ × 5″

Traditionally, appliqué of canvas has been done by raveling the threads and inserting them into the canvas as shown in the photo series beginning on page 135. Before the advent of nylon canvas, it was necessary to use this time-consuming method for every type of appliqué. Nylon canvas, time saving

FIG. 7-4b *Pattern for background.*

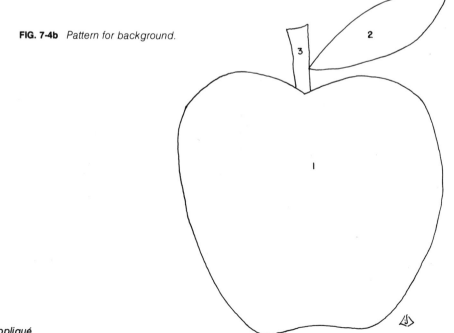

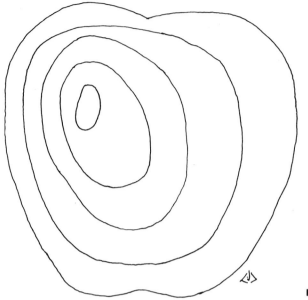

FIG. 7-4c *Pattern for Apple.*

as it is, does have limitations. It cannot be stuffed as high as the traditional method allows us, because it does not ease in readily. And it comes in just one small size (20) that I know of. Regular Mono comes in many sizes.

Stitch the apple and the background. Block (page 241). Stitch the leaf. Cut out and attach it to the canvas in the apple area, using the detached canvas method (page 88). Appliqué the apple as shown on page 135. Frame (page 247).

FIG. 7-4d *Pattern for leaf.*

8

Mixed media

This chapter shows you that many kinds of techniques can be used on one canvas to achieve the look you need. Let the following projects fire your imagination.

Needlepoint shop

STITCHES: Basketweave
                Continental (letters)
                Bargello (chair seats)

CANVAS: Silk Gauze 54, 4″ × 4″ (¼″ margins included)

YARN: Embroidery floss, one ply used; #5 pearl cotton and Persian (fern)

NEEDLE: Fine sewing needle; blunt end on concrete or metal file.

SIZE OF FINISHED PROJECT: Fills an area 3½″ × 4½″ × 1½″.

FIG. 8-1a *Needlepoint Shop.*

Even though the stitchery itself is not three-dimensional, this little Needlepoint Shop shows you how to combine two of America's most popular hobbies: miniatures and needlepoint.

The two chair seats are stitched in a Bargello pattern (Figure 8-1g) along with several preworked canvases that will be "for sale" in the shop. The shop's sign is stitched, and there is another piece in progress on the table. Work all the designs on one piece of canvas, leaving generous margins. As you can see in Figure 8-1b, not much margin was left, and Lois Ann came to regret that. (Isn't hindsight great?)

Cut the pieces of needlepoint apart. Turn the raw edges of the chair seats under, and hold them in place with a dot or two of glue. Then glue the seat covers to the miniature chair seat.

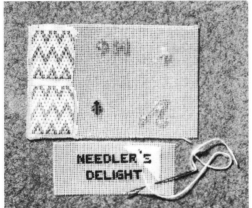

FIG. 8-1b (left) *Needlepoint pieces in Needlepoint Shop.*

FIG. 8-1c–h
Patterns for Needlepoint Shop.

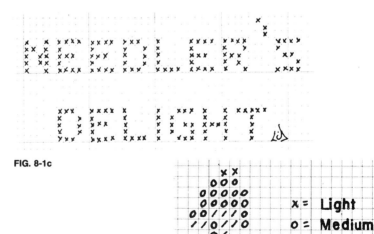

FIG. 8-1c

FIG. 8-1d

x = Light
o = Medium
/ = Dark

130

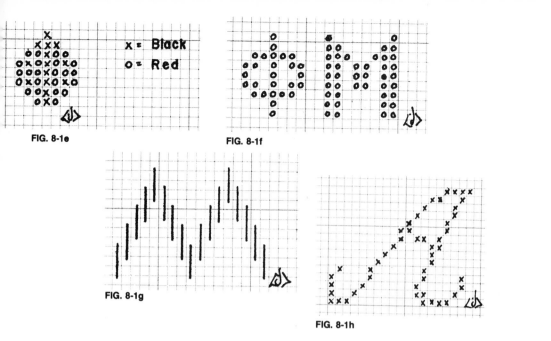

FIG. 8-1e

x = Black
o = Red

FIG. 8-1f

FIG. 8-1g

FIG. 8-1h

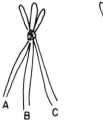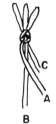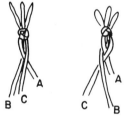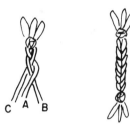

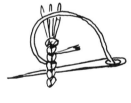

FIG. 8-1i *How to make fern.*

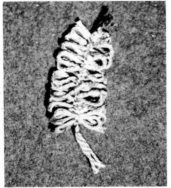

FIG. 8-1j *Finished fern stem.*

Hang the preworked canvases on the wall with a *small* dot of glue. Use a toothpick. Let the glue dry thoroughly before standing the shop upright.

Again use a small amount of glue on a toothpick to stick the sign to a piece of white posterboard. Cut a frame out of cardboard with a razor blade, and glue it in place.

The fern in the basket is made from #5 pearl cotton. Braid it in varying lengths from ¾" to 1". Thread a small needle with 1-ply Persian yarn. Pierce the braid with the needle, leaving a tail. Take a Backstitch on the braid to secure the thread. Follow Figure 8-1i to make the fern leaves. Clip the loops. Make at least eight of these stems.

Use a whole 6-ply embroidery strand instead of the 1-ply Persian for some of the leaves to add texture and variety to them. Gather them together at one end, and stitch them together with two ply of embroidery floss. Using the same thread, sew this bunch of fern stems to a circle of posterboard ½" in diameter. This will be a false bottom for the pot.

Make a pot from lightweight cardboard or stiff paper with a bottom slightly bigger than the one the fern is attached to. Cut a strip about 1¾" long and ½" deep. Roll it so that it forms a cylinder just a hair smaller than the base of the pot. Glue the side seam together. Use a paper clip to hold it until it dries. Glue the cylinder to the pot bottom. Let it dry. Put a dot of glue on the inside bottom of the pot. Put the false bottom inside the pot. Hold it in place until it dries. (Hope you're using fast-drying glue!) Hang with an embroidery floss or pearl cotton hanger. Glue it to the ceiling.

Make miniature twists of many colors of yarn from one ply of Persian yarn. Put them in a tub or display them on the wall.

The shop is a découpage box that was painted at home. Insert your miniatures into the box, and glue them in place.

STITCHES: 1. Reversed Scotch
                2. Cut Turkey Work
                3. Needleweaving
                4. Looped Turkey Work
                5. Shisha
                6. Continental
                7. Straight Stitches (whiskers, nose, ear)

CANVAS: Mono (Regular or Interlock) 10, 10½" × 13½"
(3" margins included); Regular Mono 18, 6½" for both eyes
(3" margins included)

YARN: Tapestry or Persian (for Turkey Work), gold metallic

NEEDLE: Size 18 or 20 and 22

SIZE OF FINISHED PROJECT: 4½" × 7"

Stitch the background right up to the flower centers. Attach
small mirrors (available in craft stores) with the Shisha Stitch.
Then Stitch Looped Turkey Work in a circle around one
center, and make Needleweaving petals around the other
flower centers. Stitch the cat and his nose.

    Block (page 241). Appliqué the cat's eyes onto the
canvas as shown in Figure 8-2d–k. Then make the whiskers,
and outline the cat's left ear with Straight Stitch. Attach the
jewel with the Shisha Stitch, and sew on a gold chain. Frame
(page 247).

FIG. 8-2a *Black Cat.*

FIG. 8-2b *Pattern for Black Cat.*

THE METHODS OF THREE-DIMENSIONAL NEEDLEPOINT

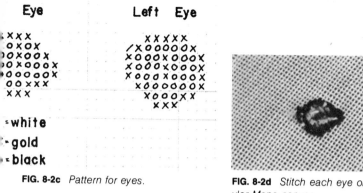

Eye

```
 XXX
 OXOX
)OXOOX
)OXOOOX
•OOOOX
 OOXXX
 XXX
```

Left Eye

```
  XXXXX
 /XOOOOOX
 XOOOXOOOX
 XOOOXOOOX
 XOOOXOOOX
 XOOOOOOX
  XOOOXX
   XXX
```

=white

'=gold

•=black

FIG. 8-2c *Pattern for eyes.*

FIG. 8-2d *Stitch each eye on Regular Mono canvas.*

FIG. 8-2e *Ravel the canvas to the stitches. Unweave any canvas that is not raveled away. I didn't here, so I found out the hard way that it's easier that way. Work the background stitch almost all the way to the area to be appliquéd.*

FIG. 8-2f *Lay the piece to be appliquéd over the area to be filled. Thread a needle with the mesh of the canvas. Insert the needle into the background canvas, and bring each of the mesh to the wrong side. More than one mesh will be inserted in each hole.*

Mixed media

135

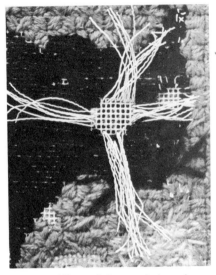

FIG. 8-2g *When all the mesh have been brought to the wrong side, it looks like this.*

FIG. 8-2h *Bury each of the mesh in the worked stitches. It's easier to bring a mesh through and bury it before you unthread the needle, but it was clearer to photograph it this way.*

FIG. 8-2i
Clip the mesh close to the canvas.

THE METHODS OF THREE-DIMENSIONAL NEEDLEPOINT

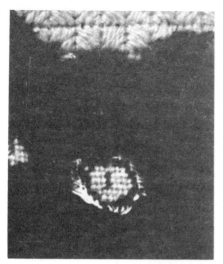

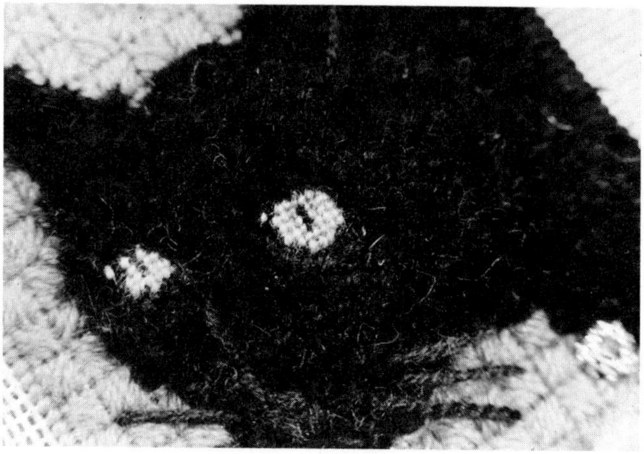

FIG. 8-2k *Now stitch the background up to the eye, following the stitch and size of stitch used for the background.*

FIG. 8-2j *When the eye is secured, it looks like this.*

City park

STITCHES:
1. Giant Cashmere
2. Continental
3. Mosaic
4. Cashmere
5. Looped Turkey Work
6. Cut Turkey Work
7. Buttonhole in Half-Circle
8. French Knots
9. Straight Stitches
10. Giant Scotch
11. Elongated Cashmere
12. Scotch
13. Backstitch (metallic)

CANVAS: Plastic 10 and 5, Interlock Mono 14 (see Figure 8-3b for sizes to cut)

YARN: Tapestry or Persian (for Cut Turkey Work); pearl cotton (#3 for popcorn cart, lake, and Cross Stitch; #1 for bushes); gold metallic (for window trim and trim on popcorn cart); rayon floss (flowers); variegated mohair (trees)

NEEDLE: Sizes 20 and 13

SIZE OF FINISHED PROJECT: 10¼" × 9¾" × 9½"

Mixed media

FIG. 8-3a-e
City Park

FIG. 8-3a

FIG. 8-3b

FIG. 8-3c

THE METHODS OF THREE-DIMENSIONAL NEEDLEPOINT

FIG. 8-3d

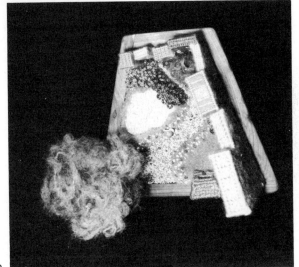

FIG. 8-3e

Stitch each piece of the buildings. Work the windows in
Continental Stitch in an orange yarn. This gives the feeling of
the setting sun reflecting off the windows. To get that extra
shine, something that reflects light needs to be added to the
needlepoint. Sylvia Fishman very generously gave me isinglass for my windows. If you cannot find isinglass, use cello-
phane, Mylar, or some other similar shiny thing. Use a tiny dot
of white glue to hold the windowpane in place while you work.
Stitch a windowpane arrangement in a gold thread that will
hold the isinglass permanently in place (like Upright Cross).
Put the buildings together with an overcast Stitch.

Mixed media

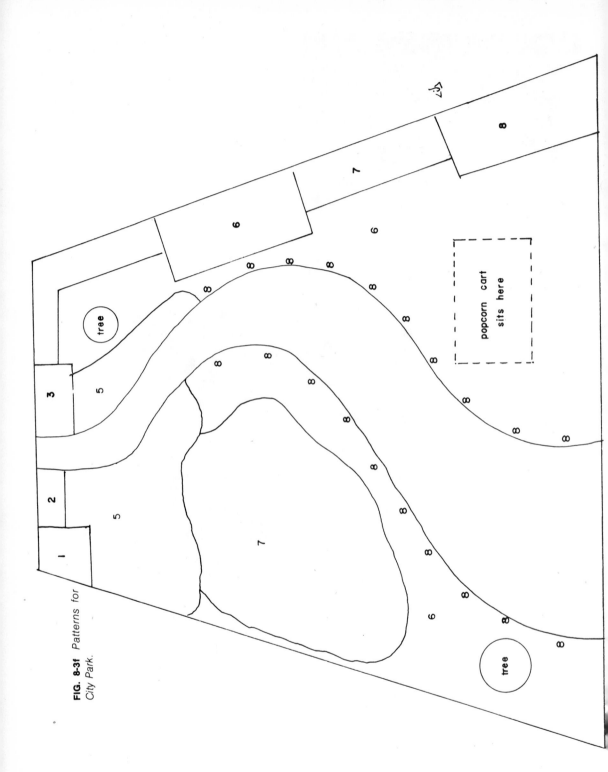

FIG. 8-3f *Patterns for City Park.*

THE METHODS OF THREE-DIMENSIONAL NEEDLEPOINT

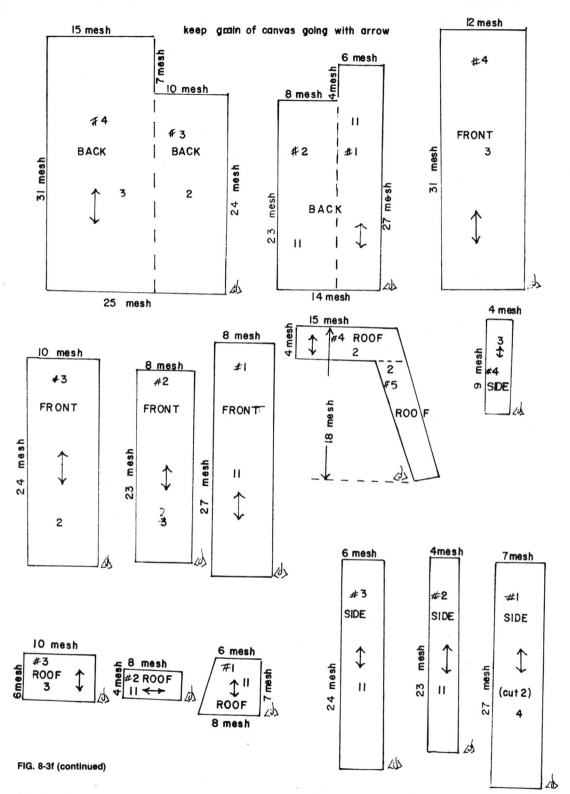

keep grain of canvas going with arrow

FIG. 8-3f (continued)

Mixed media

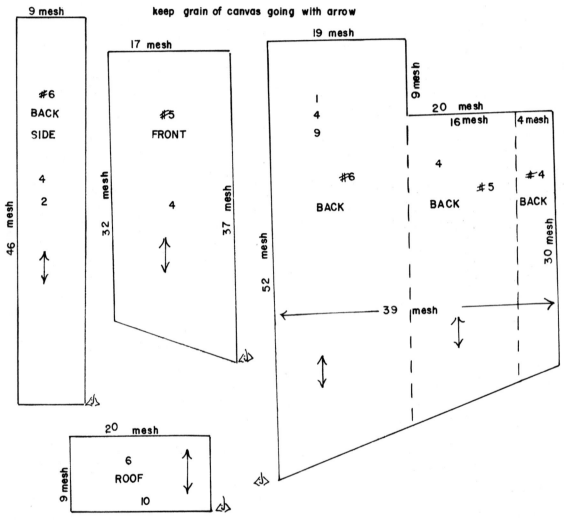

keep grain of canvas going with arrow

9 mesh

#6
BACK
SIDE

4
2

46 mesh

17 mesh

#5
FRONT

4

32 mesh

37 mesh

19 mesh

1
4
9

#6

BACK

52 mesh

9 mesh

20 mesh

16 mesh

4 mesh

4

#5

#4

BACK

BACK

16 mesh

30 mesh

39 mesh

20 mesh

6
ROOF

10

9 mesh

FIG. 8-3f (continued)

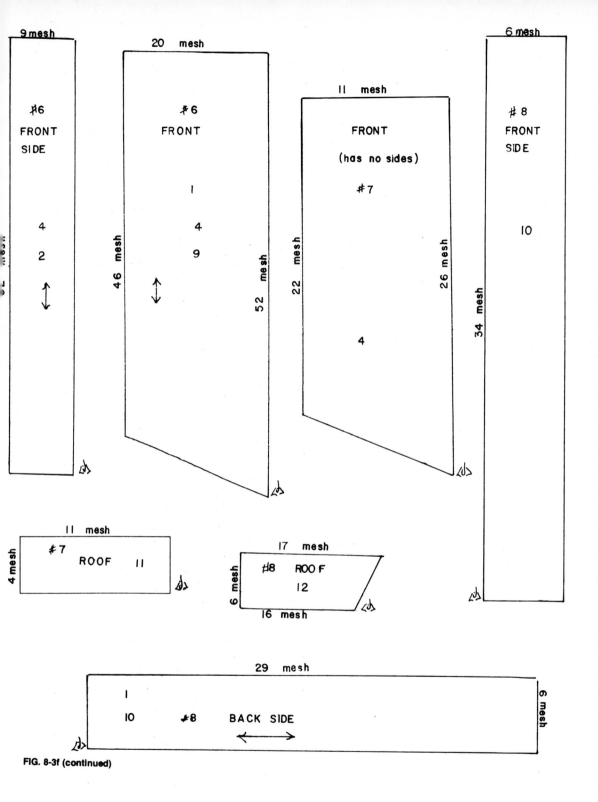

9 mesh

#6
FRONT
SIDE

4

2

20 mesh

#6
FRONT

1

4

9

46 mesh

52 mesh

11 mesh

FRONT
(has no sides)

#7

4

22 mesh

26 mesh

6 mesh

#8
FRONT
SIDE

10

34 mesh

11 mesh

#7   ROOF   11

4 mesh

17 mesh

#8   ROOF

12

6 mesh

16 mesh

29 mesh

1

10   #8   BACK SIDE

6 mesh

FIG. 8-3f (continued)

Mixed media

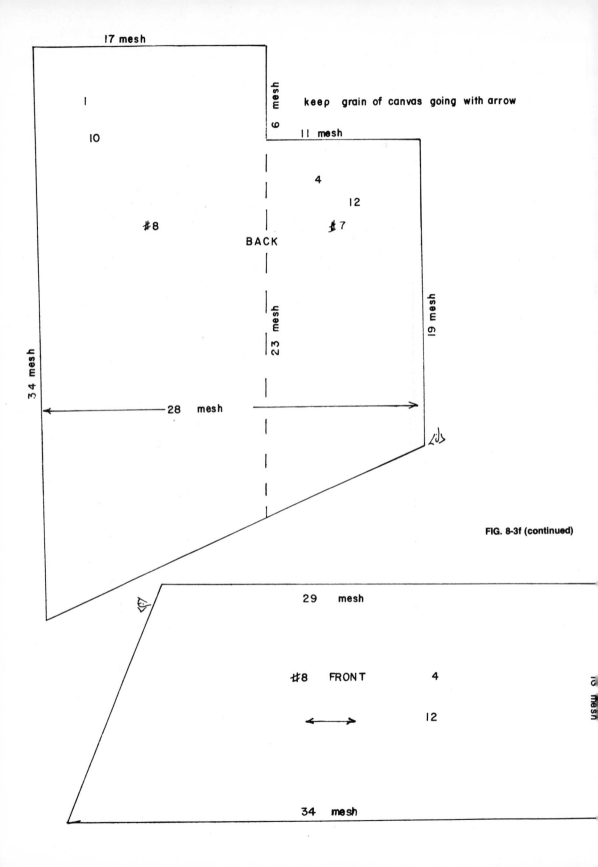

17 mesh

I

10

6 mesh

keep grain of canvas going with arrow

11 mesh

4

12

#8

#7

BACK

23 mesh

19 mesh

34 mesh

28 mesh

FIG. 8-3f (continued)

29 mesh

#8 FRONT 4

12

34 mesh

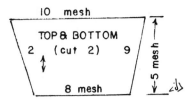

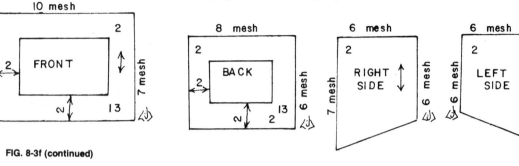

FIG. 8-3f (continued)

It's hard to get the plastic canvas covered when putting things like this together. You may need to thicken your yarn. If the canvas still shows, paint it with acrylic paint. (The paint does chip off this canvas but only as it is handled. So when you've finished stitching and handling the canvas, the paint should last.)

Stitch the grass and the lake, leaving the path blank. Next stitch the bushes. The #1 pearl cotton is a tight squeeze on Mono 14 canvas, but it can be done. Skip every other mesh and every other row in working Looped Turkey Work. Use three fingers to size the loops for the front bushes. Use two fingers to make the loops for the back bushes. Make the flowers along the path with rayon floss. Use a full strand for the front flowers, and gradually thin your yarn to two ply for the back flowers. Make the French Knots loose enough to sit on top of the grass.

Sew the buildings to the ground canvas with a Whipstitch. Stretch the ground canvas over a piece of ¼" plywood, which is the same size and shape as the ground canvas. Glue birdseed to the path for gravel. *Don't* use too much glue. I did, and the rayon floss absorbed the extra, dulling it. Insert the plywood into a pretty wooden base. Make your own, or order from the address on page 262.

Cut a dowel ½" in diameter and 6½" long. Glue brown pipe cleaners to it, so that the pipe cleaners stick out to form

Mixed media

branches (see Figure 8-3c). Glue them around the dowel so that they touch each other. Fill in the bottom of the dowel solidly with pieces of pipe cleaner. Use rubber bands to hold them in place while the glue dries. Carefully wrap brown yarn (preferably uncut) around and around and around the tree trunk and around each "branch." Bend the pipe cleaners into branchlike positions. Loosely wrap mohair yarn around each branch as shown in Figure 8-3h.

Repeat the process to make the smaller tree in the back—only start with a dowel ¼" in diameter and 1¾" long.

Drill holes at an angle in the plywood board where the trees should go. Drill right through the needlepoint and all. Insert the trees, and secure them with glue. The trees must sit in the base at the same angle the buildings do.

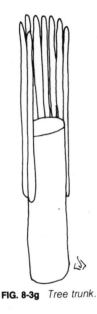

FIG. 8-3g *Tree trunk.*

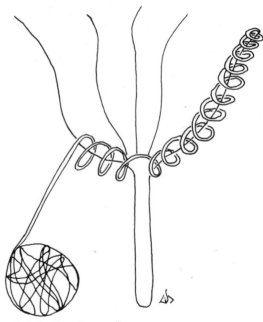

FIG. 8-3h *Tree "leaves."*

Make the popcorn cart, and put it together with an Overcast Stitch. Use the centers of four pieces of round canvas (pictured on page 8) for the wheels. Cut only the smallest circles for the two back wheels and the next biggest ones for the two front ones. Attach the wheels to the front and back pieces with a Cross Stitch. Just put the popcorn cart in place on the lawn.

The boy is a plastic one I found in a craft and hobby shop. He had one straight leg, so I sawed it off at the knee with my tomato knife! I then glued the lower leg to the grass

THE METHODS OF THREE-DIMENSIONAL NEEDLEPOINT

near the lake. When it dried. I glued the rest of the boy in place. I did make certain, however, that a flower hid most of the kid's broken knee. The raft is a piece of thin balsa wood ¼″ × ¼″ with a piece of toothpick for a mast. The sail is a triangle of white typing paper. All the parts were glued together, and then the raft was glued to the water at the center of the circles on the lake.

Northwest autumn

STITCHES: 1. Basketweave (foreground)
                 2. Straight Stitch (background)
                 3. French Knots (scattered in background)
                 4. Raised Buttonhole (bark)

CANVAS: Interlock Mono 7, 16″ × 23½″ (3″ margins included)

YARN: Persian, mohair, curly mohair

NEEDLE: Size 16

SIZE OF FINISHED PROJECT: 10″ × 15½″ × 2″

Paint the design on canvas. Stitch the background, improvising as you go. Stitch the foreground, in warm oranges, browns, and greens. Mix the orange and brown plies to give a tweedy effect. Stitches placed at random will help you to impart a feeling of dried, fall-colored leaves that have fallen on brown pine needles and green moss.

Using cooler golds, oranges, and greens, stitch the background in Straight Stitches placed horizontally across the canvas. Start at the bottom of the background with the warm golds and oranges, and progress to cooler golds and oranges. This will give a feeling of a receding background. Arrange the greens to resemble tree and bush shapes in the background. Use browns to make tree trunks—some in front of and some behind the trees. Use Raised Buttonhole Stitch. Stitch right over the background for the trees. Let your imagination guide you. Stitch the two top portions in Basketweave.

Use French Knots in golds as accents and to help hold the long Straight Stitches in place.

Block. When the needlepoint is dry, attach it to the working frame. Start from the bottom, and work up. Using a

FIG. 8-4a *Northwest Autumn.*

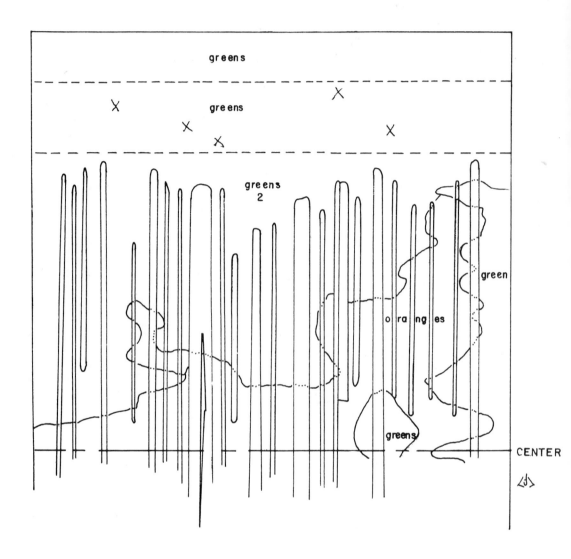

greens

greens

greens
2

green

oranges

greens

CENTER

X Marks spot where wrapped yarn trees are attached.

FIG. 8-4b *Pattern for Northwest Autumn.*

X — Marks spot where wrapped yarn trees are attached.

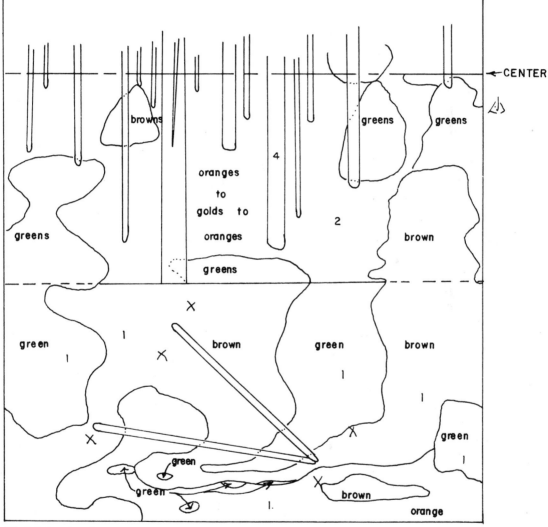

FIG. 8-4b (continued)

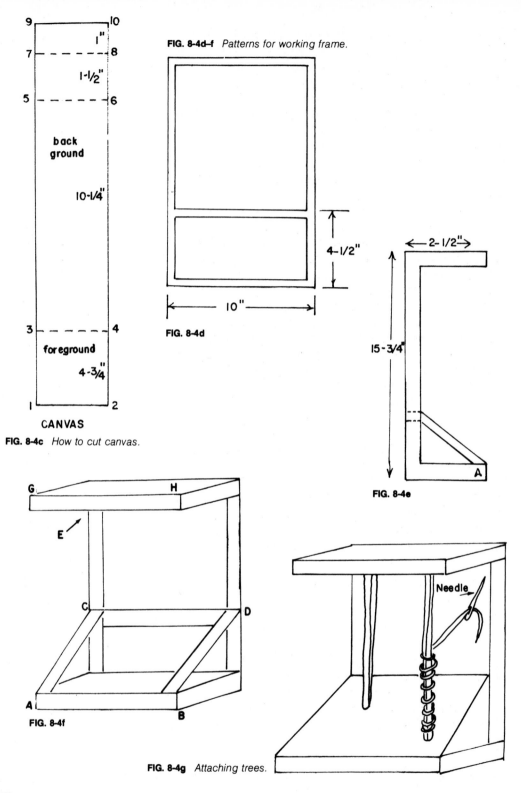

9 ⎡⎻⎻⎻⎻⎻⎻⎻⎤ 10
      1"
7 ⎢- - - - -⎢ 8

      1-1/2"

5 ⎢- - - - -⎢ 6

    back
    ground

    10-1/4"

3 ⎢- - - - -⎢ 4

    foreground

    4-3/4"

1 ⎣⎻⎻⎻⎻⎻⎻⎻⎦ 2

CANVAS

FIG. 8-4c *How to cut canvas.*

FIG. 8-4d–f *Patterns for working frame.*

4–1/2"

10"

FIG. 8-4d

← 2–1/2" →

15–3/4"

A

FIG. 8-4e

G   H

E

C   D

A   B

FIG. 8-4f

Needle

FIG. 8-4g *Attaching trees.*

150

staple gun, staple the bottom line of the needlepoint (line 1–2 in Figure 8-4c) from A to B in Figure 8-4f. Move the Straight Stitches aside at line 3–4 (Figure 8–4c), and staple it along line C–D on the frame in Figure 8-4f. Pull the yarns back in place to cover the staples. Staple line 5–6 (Figure 8-4c) along E–F (Figure 8-4f), moving yarns as you did before. Finally staple line 9–10 (Figure 8-4c) on line G–H (Figure 8-4f). No bare wood should show now. Turn the bare canvas around the sides of the frame. Miter the corners as shown on page 251. Carefully clip the canvas at points E and F, and turn to the back and staple. Put a dot of white glue along the edges of the cut canvas.

You are now ready to make the five trees that stand free of the canvas. Secure your yarn at the top and bottom of the top and foreground sections of the canvas. String several strands together between the top and bottom of the canvas (Figure 8-4g). Stagger the placement of the trees. Wrap yarn around and around and around and around the basic structure for the trunks. Mix browns with a light touch of oranges. Wrap evenly, making the bases of the trunks larger than the tops.

Use the same procedure to make two fallen trees on the ground.

Using green mohair, loosely arrange it around the trunks in clusters, so that it resembles pine trees. Tack it lightly in place on the trunks, on the background canvas, and at the top.

Loosely arrange the gold curly mohair on the ground to look like fallen leaves. Tack it in place.

Have the piece professionally framed. It might help your framer to tell him or her that two moldings can be put together to make a suitable shadowbox frame. The inside of the sides can be hidden with brown mat board.

Waste knot, want knot

This project is included here to inspire you to go on to projects of your own. The instructions on how to make this piece are not included for obvious reasons. You could never find a real knothole exactly like this one. So the Bargello pattern for this piece is irrelevant. However, you could make a similar piece around your own knot or driftwood with your own Bargello pattern. Let this idea guide you.

The hole for the knot is about ½" smaller all the way

around. This allows a ¼" hem and some overlap to hold the found object in. Vary the size of the stitches and the wave of the rows to simulate the grain of wood. You can use the same technique to simulate the ripples of sand and/or water. Use shells or coral as your found objects. Let your imagination go wild!

I hope this trip through three-dimensional needlepoint has taught you several things: (1) Never be afraid of your canvas. (2) Use supplies that do the job—whether or not it's a traditional use for them. (3) Have fun!

FIG. 8-5 *Waste Knot, Want Knot.*

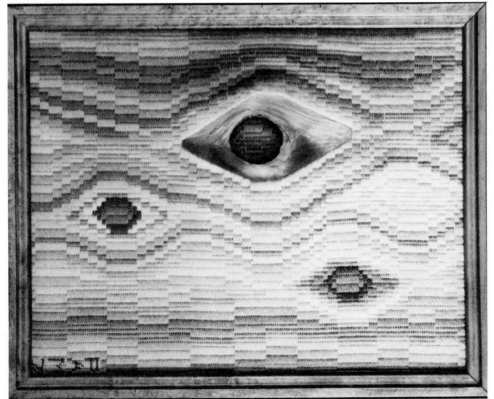

THE METHODS OF THREE-DIMENSIONAL NEEDLEPOINT

THE STITCHES

How to read the diagrams

Before you even start to stitch, you will need to know the definition of the symbols used in the drawings. ⟨·J⟩ shows the location of the beginning of the stitch. In stitches that are done in steps, the starts are identified by ⟨·J⟩1, ⟨·J⟩ A, ⟨·J⟩ a, ⟨·J⟩ AA, and ⟨·J⟩ aa, in that order.

Arrows alone indicate a row change with no turning of the canvas. Arrows accompanied by a clock show a turning of the canvas:

T   🕒   means: "Turn 90° to the right."

T   🕕   means: "Turn 180°."

T   🕘   means: "Turn 90° to the left."

Where it would complicate things, these arrows and clocks have been omitted. However, you can still tell where to turn the canvas. Simply turn the book so that the numbers are upright. Turn your canvas the same way, and stitch.

When several stitches go into the same hole, the numbers have been omitted, because there simply is not room for all of them. (See the Eye Stitches, pages 205–208.)

The numbering has been arranged so that the best backing is created. Economical yarn usage usually creates a poor backing. This poor backing reduces the durability of needlepoint.

A change of color is indicated by darkening the stitches, but the use of a second color is not absolutely necessary. This darkening also helps you to see the next row more clearly. Other colors (third, fourth, etc.) are indicated by different designs within each stitch. When working with two colors that cross each other, put the darker color on the bottom. Work the lighter colors last.

The canvas pictured is the canvas used for the particular stitch. Generally, all stitches can be worked on Penelope canvas; Regular Mono canvas does have some restrictions on types of stitches that can be used. These are pictured on Penelope canvas. (These restrictions do not exist on Interlock Mono canvas.) The rest of the stitches have been drawn on Mono canvas for simplicity and clarity.

Chapter

9

Straight stitches

Straight Stitches are those stitches that cover the canvas vertically or horizontally. A vertical stitch covers 2 to 6 horizontal mesh and lies entirely between 2 vertical mesh. A horizontal stitch covers 2 to 6 vertical mesh and lies entirely between 2 horizontal mesh.

A single strand of both tapestry and Persian yarn, when worked in Straight Stitches, covers Mono 14 canvas well. On Penelope or Mono 10 or 12, you will have to thicken your yarn.

Straight Stitches make beautiful patterns and make a good background (as a rule). They work up quickly and can give a good backing if you plan on it.

Most of the Straight Stitches depend on color for their splendor.

Straight Stitches do not distort the canvas when you stitch. I recommend Straight Stitches for beginners.

Take a Bargello Tuck as you bury the tail (page 23).

If you wish to mix Straight Stitches with Diagonal Stitches, you can refer to page 28 for directions.

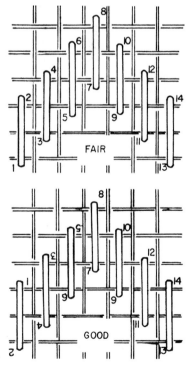

FIG. 9-1 *Making good backing.*

STRAIGHT STITCHES

	BORDER	GOOD BACKING	POOR BACKING	BACKGROUND	DESIGN	ACCENT	FAST	SLOW	GEOMETRIC PATTERN	SHADING	YARN HOG	SNAGS	SNAGPROOF	LITTLE TEXTURE	MEDIUM TEXTURE	HIGH RELIEF	FLOWER STITCH	WEAK PATTERN	MEDIUM PATTERN	STRONG PATTERN	DISTORTS CANVAS
STRAIGHT GOBELIN (see p. 157)	•	•		•	•				•				•	•				•			
STRAIGHT STITCH (see p. 157)		•			•		•					•		•				•			
SPLIT GOBELIN (see p. 158)		•		•	•				•	•	•		•	•				•			
BRICK (see p. 158)		•		•	•				•	•			•	•				•			
GIANT BRICK (see p. 159)		•		•	•		•		•	•			•	•					•		
DOUBLE BRICK (see p. 159)		•		•	•		•		•					•					•		
HORIZONTAL BRICK (see p. 160)		•		•	•		•		•	•			•	•					•		
SHINGLE (see p. 160)		•		•	•		•							•					•		
HUNGARIAN (see p. 161)	•	•		•	•	•	•		•					•					•		
F-106 (see p. 161)	•	•		•	•	•	•		•			•		•						•	
BARGELLO LINE PATTERN (see p. 163)		•		•	•		•		•	•		•		•						•	
BARGELLO FRAMEWORK PATTERN (see p. 164)		•		•	•		•		•	•		•		•						•	

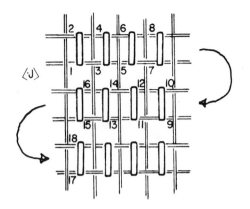

FIG. 9-2

Straight stitch

I've used this term to indicate any stitch that is taken by placing thread or yarn between point A and point B. It may take several stitches laid side by side to fill the area (actually Satin Stitch), or it may take several stitches in different directions to create the desired effect. The Long Stitch is also a Straight Stitch.

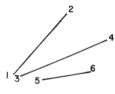

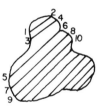

FIG. 9-3

Split gobelin

FIG. 9-4

This stitch is based on embroidery's Split Stitch. It is particularly good for shading. Work this stitch over 2 to 5 mesh.

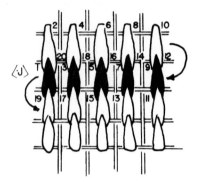

Brick

FIG. 9-5

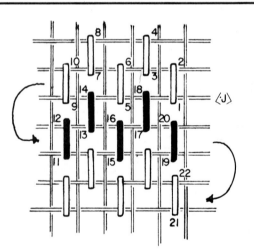

This stitch may be worked over 4 or 6 mesh with an even step (see page 162).

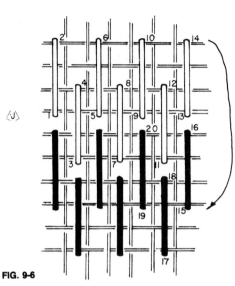

⟨J⟩

FIG. 9-6

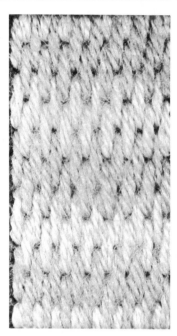

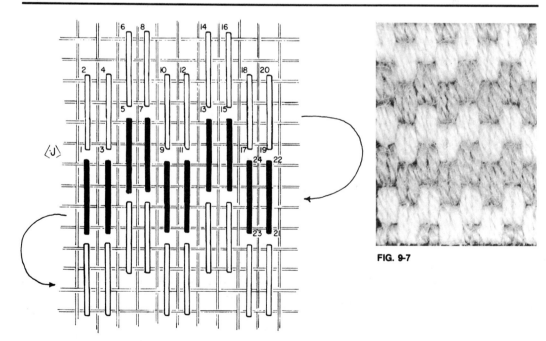

⟨J⟩

FIG. 9-7

Horizontal brick

This stitch can be worked over 2 or 4 mesh.

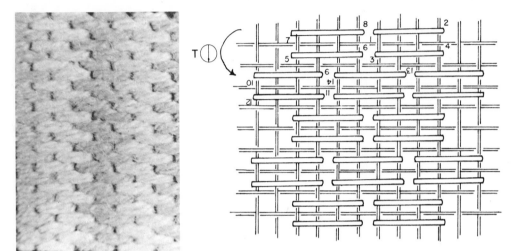

Shingle

This arrangement of Straight Stitches reminds me of shingles on a roof.

FIG. 9-9

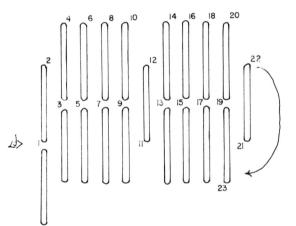

This vertical stitch establishes a diamond pattern. It is good in two colors, although it is stunning in one color. It is a set of three stitches—2:4:2. Skip a space. Repeat 2:4:2. Skip a space under the long stitch. Continue the pattern—2:4:2, then skip, then 2:4:2, etc.

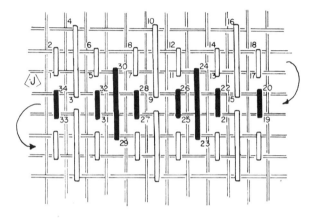

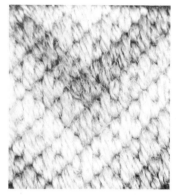

FIG. 9-10

F-106

Various color combinations make this stitch look different.

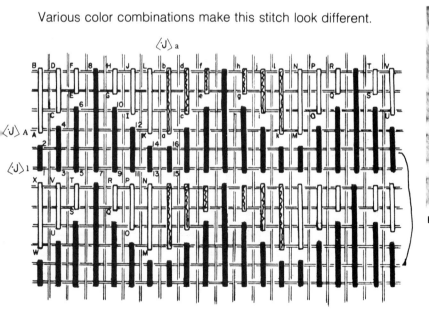

FIG. 9-11

Bargello

Bargello is Straight Stitches worked in a geometric pattern. These stitches can vary in size from 2 mesh tall to 6 mesh tall. When stitches are placed next to each other in a zigzag line, the distance between the *top* of one stitch and the *top* of the next one is called a *step*. It is referred to by number—for example, "4:2." The "4" indicates how many mesh tall the stitch is; the "2" tells us how many mesh in the step. A "4:2" stitch is the most common in Bargello. The smaller the step number is, the more gradual the incline (a). The larger the step number is, the steeper the incline (c).

A line pattern is a zigzag line of stitches. Both the stitch size and the step number may vary within one line.

To produce arcs or curves, place more than one stitch in the same step (4:0). The more stitches there are on one step, the broader the curve (d).

These arcs or curves may be combined with a zigzag line for a more interesting pattern.

A framework pattern can be made by turning a line

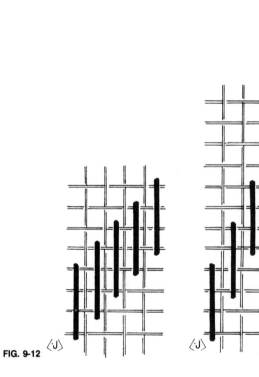
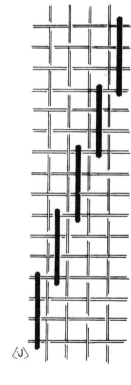

FIG. 9-12

pattern upside down (see page 164). Fill the center in with a secondary pattern of your choice.

Bargello has limitless variations, both in stitch and in color. There is much more to learn about Bargello. There are many other kinds of patterns. Refer to any of the many good books on Bargello.

Note: In working a whole piece in Bargello, start the pattern in the middle of the canvas to achieve balance.

Bargello line pattern

This is an example only. Both stitch size and step number may vary within one line.

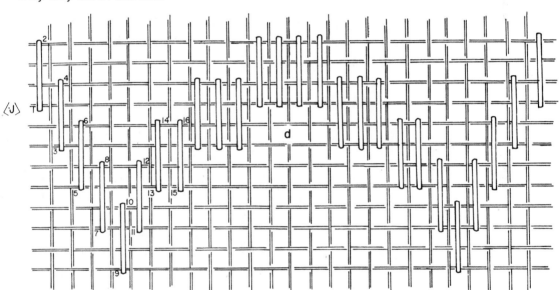

FIG. 9-13

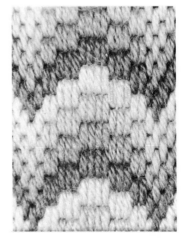

Bargello framework pattern

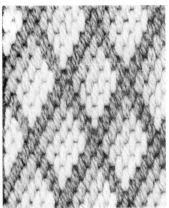

FIG. 9-14

Try working the framework in the darkest color and shading the center. This is an example only.

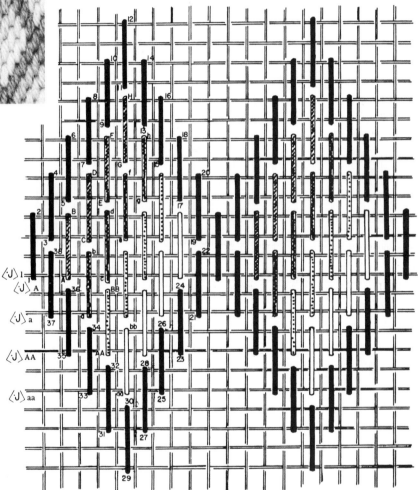

Diagonal stitches

Diagonal Stitches are those that cover the canvas by crossing junctions of mesh rather than going between them. In referring to these slanted stitches, I have designated the angle or slant they take by two numbers. The first number refers to the number of mesh that you go up or down. The second number refers to the number of mesh that you go over. For example, a 1 × 1 stitch is a Tent Stitch; 1 × 3, 3 × 1, and 3 × 3 stitches are illustrated. For those stitches where both numbers are the same, you may count diagonally the junctions of mesh instead of counting up 3 and over 3. Whether you go up or down (for the first number) is shown in the sketch that accompanies each stitch.

Mono or Penelope 10 canvas usually accepts one strand of tapestry or Persian yarn for Diagonal Stitches.

Tent Stitches are Basketweave, Continental, and Half Cross.

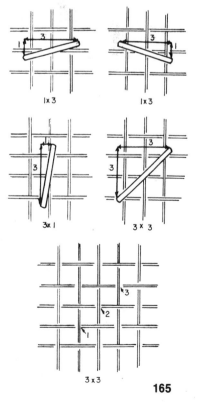

1x3 1x3

3x1 3x3

FIG. 10-1

3x3

DIAGONAL STITCHES

	BORDER	GOOD BACKING	POOR BACKING	BACKGROUND	DESIGN	ACCENT	FAST	SLOW	GEOMETRIC PATTERN	SHADING	YARN HOG	SNAGS	SNAGPROOF	LITTLE TEXTURE	MEDIUM TEXTURE	HIGH RELIEF	FLOWER STITCH	WEAK PATTERN	MEDIUM PATTERN	STRONG PATTERN	DISTORTS CANVAS
BASKETWEAVE (see p. 167)		•		•	•								•	•				•			
CONTINENTAL (see p. 169)		•			•					•			•	•				•			•
HALF CROSS (see p. 171)			•										•	•				•			•
PETIT POINT (see p. 172)		•		•	•	•			•		•		•	•				•			•
SLANTED GOBELIN 2 x 2 (see p. 173)	•	•		•	•		•		•					•					•		•
SPLIT SLANTED GOBELIN (see p. 173)		•		•	•			•		•			•	•				•			•
INTERLOCKING GOBELIN (see p. 174)		•		•	•			•		•				•				•			•
LAZY KALEM (see p. 174)		•		•	•								•	•				•			
STEM (see p. 175)	•	•		•	•									•					•		
BYZANTINE #1 (see p. 176)		•		•	•		•		•		•			•						•	•
BYZANTINE #3 (see p. 177)		•		•	•		•				•			•						•	•
ORIENTAL (see p. 178)		•		•	•	•					•			•						•	•

Basketweave

Basketweave is one of the most used and misused stitches in needlepoint. It is an excellent stitch to know and use. A durable backing, resembling a woven pattern, is created. This makes it a "must" for chairs, footstools, and other items that will receive lots of wear.

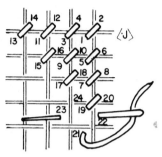

FIG. 10-2

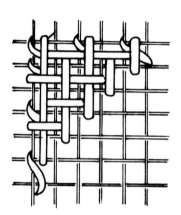

Last row is DOWN row.

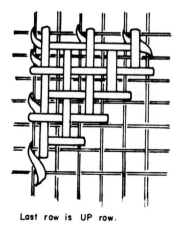

Last row is UP row.

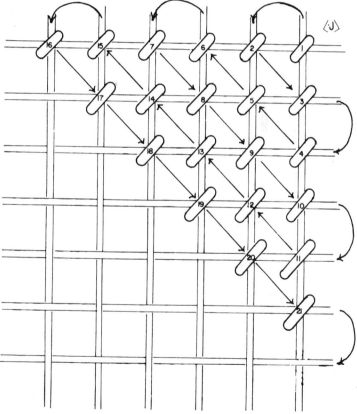

167

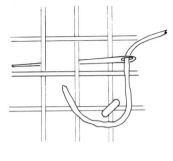

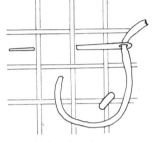

FIG. 10-2 (continued)

The finished piece is not distorted but still needs blocking (see page 241). Basketweave allows a worked canvas to give a lot, yet still be strong. It can be worked without turning the canvas. Because it lacks maneuverability, it is not a good stitch for designing. (Use Continental for designing in very small areas if you want a Tent Stitch.)

Study the illustration of the sequence of stitches on page 167. Note that, basically, the stitch fills the canvas in diagonal rows, starting at the upper right corner.

As you work, you will notice that a pattern is developing. In making an up row, the needle always goes straight across under 2 mesh. In making a down row, the needle always goes straight down under 2 mesh. Notice that the first of these 2 mesh is covered by a stitch in the preceding row. It is a very common error to go across or under 3 mesh by not counting the covered one.

At the end of each row, there is what many students refer to as a *turn stitch*. Actually it is the first stitch of a new row. If it helps you to consider it a turn stitch, then do so. At the end of the up row, this is a horizontal Continental Stitch, and at the end of the down row, this is a vertical Continental Stitch. The common error here is to leave the turn stitch out. Often students get carried away and make two turn stitches. If you have made an error somewhere, check to see if this is it.

When your yarn runs out and you must start another yarn, be sure to start *exactly* where you left off. If you do not, a line will show on the right side. For example, if your yarn runs out at the end of an up row, do not start the new yarn at the bottom of that up row you just finished, thus starting another up row. Instead you should be at the top of that last up row, ready to begin a down row. Most people tend to put their work away for the day when they have finished working the yarn on the needle. It might help you not to do this when working Basketweave. Leave the needle threaded with half a yarn, and stick it into the canvas in position ready to take the next stitch. This way, you will not lose your place. (This is illustrated on page 167.)

When working Basketweave on Regular Mono canvas, note that at the intersections of mesh in a horizontal row, the vertical mesh alternate between being on top of and underneath the horizontal mesh. However, on the diagonal, the vertical mesh are always on top or underneath the horizontal mesh. If you take care always to cover the vertical mesh intersections with a down row and to cover the horizontal mesh intersections with an up row, you will produce a stitch that is very even in appearance on the right side. This will also help you to keep track of up rows and down rows (see the illustrations).

When you come to the end of each strand of yarn, weave it under the yarns on the back side of the canvas for about an inch. Follow the weave that the stitch makes. Clip closely. This will keep the back neat. If you work the beginning and ending tails under any other way, a ridge will form that will show on the right side.

Basketweave is not really frightfully complicated. It may take some study on your part, but once you get the hang of the stitch, you will enjoy working it. It has a certain rhythm that develops easily. You can achieve a perfection with this stitch that is unique. Use it no matter how small the area. (When the area is absolutely too small and when outlining, use the Continental Stitch.)

Continental

The Continental Stitch has the next best backing, and it is the next most distinct stitch of the Tent Stitches. Its main drawback is that it pulls the canvas badly out of shape.

You really should use Basketweave wherever you can. But Continental will get the very small areas that Basketweave cannot.

FIG. 10-3

Continental: Horizontal—
work left to right

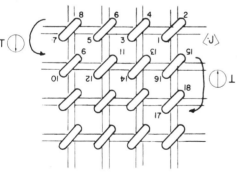

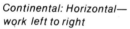

Continental: Reverse side

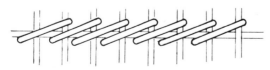

Diagonal stitches

Continental: Vertical—work down

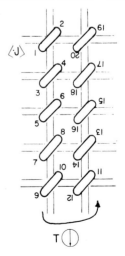

If you insist on using Continental instead of Basketweave, you should try to make the stitches as even and uniform as possible. You may work Continental either horizontally or vertically, as illustrated. Choose the direction that best fills the area you have. Work the stitch in that direction—for the whole space. Combinations of horizontally and vertically worked Continental will produce lines on the right side. Always work this stitch from right to left. If you are filling a large space, do not turn the canvas upside down for the second row; cut the yarn, and begin the second row below the first on the right. The drawings do not show this, because I do not recommend that you use this stitch in a large enough area to matter.

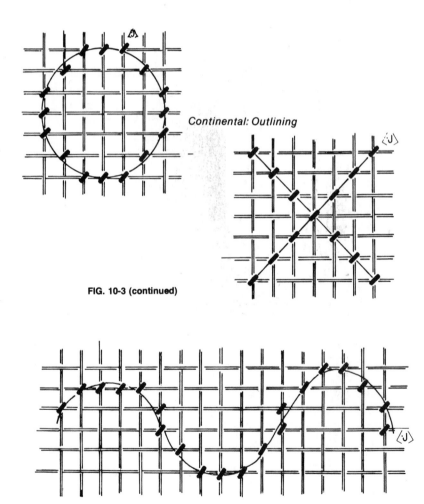

Continental: Outlining

FIG. 10-3 (continued)

Use Half Cross only when the backing of the Continental is in your way.

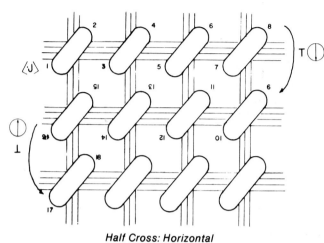

Half Cross: Horizontal

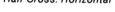

FIG. 10-4

Half Cross: Reverse side

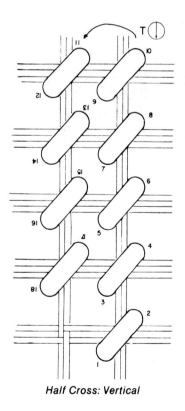

Half Cross: Vertical

Petit point

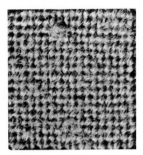

FIG. 10-5

Split the vertical mesh of Penelope canvas, and work Continental or Basketweave. Thin your yarn. This is difficult to get smooth and even on Penelope canvas. Use it only if one or two small areas of your design demand Petit Point. For a whole Petit Point picture, use Petit Point canvas (page 8). Most of the stitches in this book can be worked in Petit Point, too.

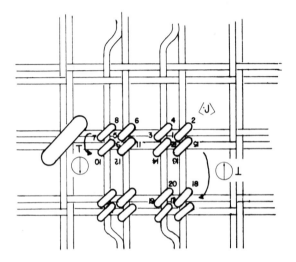

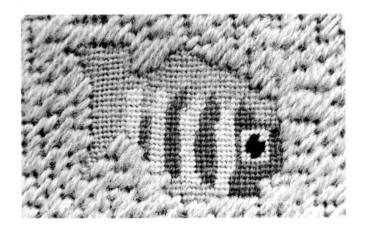

Slanted gobelin 2 x 2

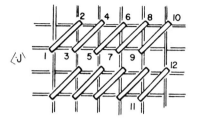

FIG. 10-6

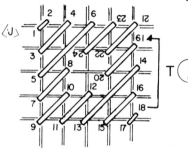

Split slanted gobelin

This stitch is reminiscent of embroidery's Split Stitch. Use it for shading. It is tedious to work but very pretty. It also does well for bird feathers.

FIG. 10-7

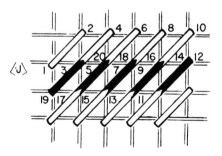

Interlocking gobelin

FIG. 10-8

This stitch is similar to Split Gobelin. However, it does not split the stitch on the row above; the second row's stitches merely rest beside the first row's stitches. It, too, can be worked 2 to 5 mesh tall and 1 to 2 wide.

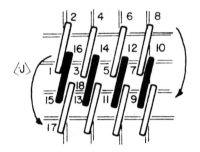

Lazy kalem

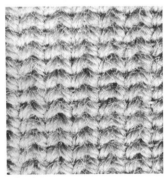

FIG. 10-9

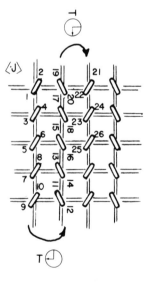

THE STITCHES

The Stem Stitch is usually best with two colors. Use a thinner yarn for the Backstitch. Complete one column of stitches at a time. Do a vertical Backstitch in a second color between the columns. This stitch makes good fences, columns, etc.

FIG. 10-10

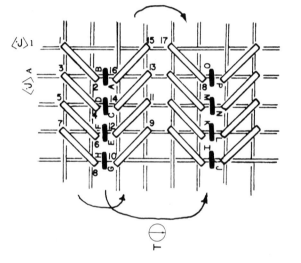

Byzantine #1

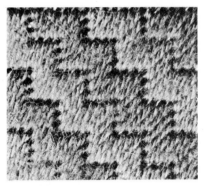

FIG. 10-11

Byzantine makes good steps and fills in diagonally shaped areas well. (Take a Bargello Tuck, page 23.)

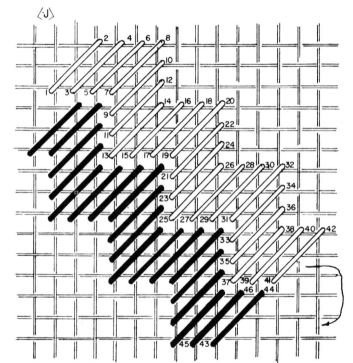

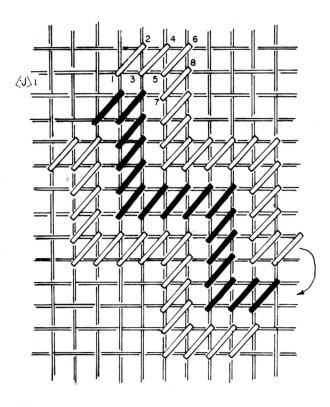

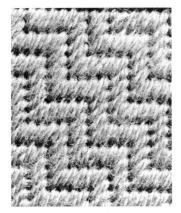

FIG. 10-12

Oriental

FIG. 10-13

The Oriental Stitch is good background in one color. It looks entirely different in two colors. Few stitches undergo such a change in appearance. Try it both ways.

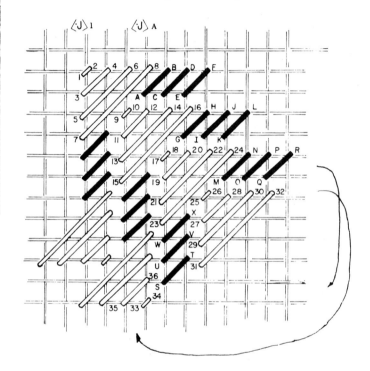

Box stitches

Box Stitches are a series of diagonal stitches that form squares or boxes. The diagonal Box Stitches are simply boxes laid in a diagonal line with the corners overlapping. (See the Diagonal Cashmere Stitch, page 186.) Note how the short stitch is shared.

Most of these stitches make excellent borders. They lend themselves to beautiful geometric patterns in several colors. I have only gone into a few color variations, for there are whole books that discuss color variations on just a few stitches.

The Box Stitch sampler was worked on Penelope 10, although it could have been done on Mono 10 canvas. Tapestry yarn was used throughout—and for all of these stitches, I did not have to thicken or thin the yarn.

BOX STITCHES

	BORDER	GOOD BACKING	POOR BACKING	BACKGROUND	DESIGN	ACCENT	FAST	SLOW	GEOMETRIC PATTERN	SHADING	YARN HOG	SNAGS	SNAGPROOF	LITTLE TEXTURE	MEDIUM TEXTURE	HIGH RELIEF	FLOWER STITCH	WEAK PATTERN	MEDIUM PATTERN	STRONG PATTERN	DISTORTS CANVAS
MOSAIC (see p. 181)	•	•		•	•		•		•				•	•				•			•
REVERSED MOSAIC (see p. 182)	•	•		•	•		•		•				•	•				•			
DIAGONAL MOSAIC (see p. 182)		•		•	•		•		•	•			•	•				•			•
CASHMERE (see p. 183)	•	•		•	•		•		•				•	•				•			•
FRAMED CASHMERE (see p. 184)	•	•		•	•				•				•	•						•	•
ELONGATED CASHMERE (see p. 185)	•	•		•	•		•		•				•	•				•			•
DIAGONAL CASHMERE (see p. 186)		•		•	•		•		•	•			•	•						•	•
SCOTCH (see p. 187)	•	•		•	•		•		•					•				•			•
GIANT SCOTCH (see p. 188)	•	•		•	•		•		•		•			•				•			•
TIED SCOTCH (see p. 189)	•	•			•	•			•				•		•				•		•
FRAMED SCOTCH (see p. 190)	•	•		•	•		•		•											•	•
REVERSED SCOTCH (see p. 191)	•	•		•	•		•		•					•				•			

Mosaic

Mosaic is the smallest of the Box Stitches. It is just 3 diagonal stitches: short, long, short. It makes a box 2 by 2 mesh. Mosaic is an excellent background or design stitch. This stitch is a good background to work behind Continental letters. It can be worked horizontally, vertically, or diagonally.

FIG. 11-1

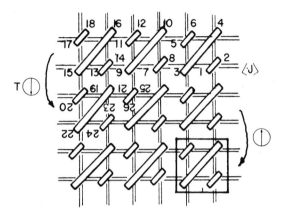

Mosaic: Horizontal

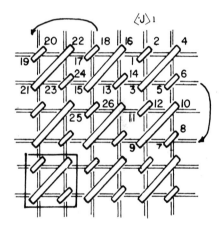

Mosaic: Diagonal

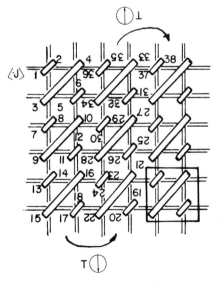

Mosaic: Vertical

Reversed mosaic

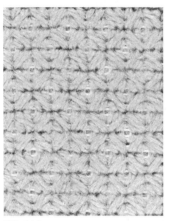

FIG. 11-2

This stitch is worked most easily by doing a diagonal row from upper left to lower right. Then turn the canvas 90° so that the upper right now becomes the upper left. Work the same type of diagonal row, filling in the blank spaces. I think this stitch looks best in one color.

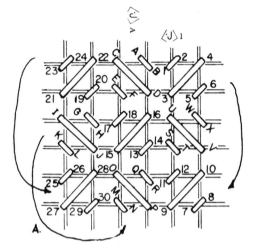

Diagonal mosaic

FIG. 11-3

When Mosaic is worked diagonally, it becomes merely a line of short and long stitches. For this reason, you may use it for shading. Do this stitch in one or more colors.

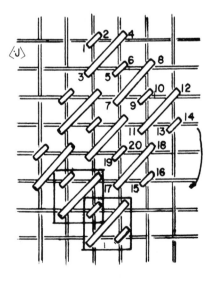

Cashmere

Cashmere is a rectangular Mosaic Stitch. It can be worked horizontally, vertically, or diagonally.

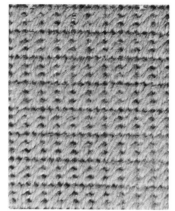

FIG. 11-4

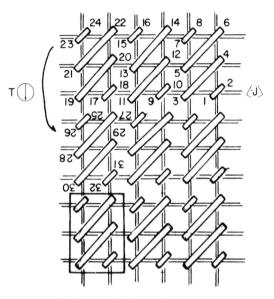

Cashmere: Horizontal

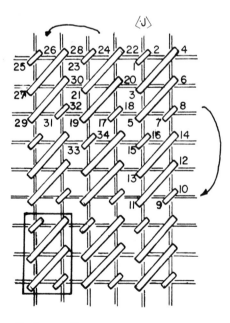

Cashmere: Diagonal

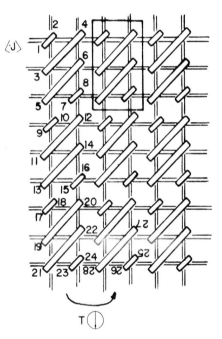

Cashmere: Vertical

Framed cashmere

FIG. 11-5

The Continental Stitch is used between the Cashmere boxes.

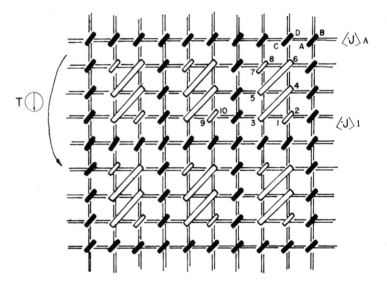

Elongated Cashmere is just an extra-long Cashmere box. In alternating rows, it reminds me of the outside of a barn. The number of long stitches may vary.

FIG. 11-6

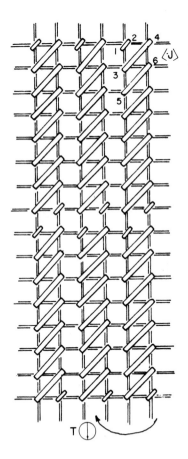

Diagonal cashmere

The second row of Diagonal Cashmere is a bit tricky to work. I try to remember that the first long stitch in the second row is diagonally below the last short stitch. After I have taken that stitch, I go back and pick up the first short stitch in the second row.

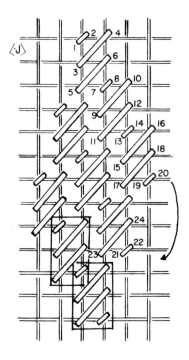

The Scotch Stitch is merely a large Mosaic Stitch. It has many lovely variations. This stitch can be worked three ways. (See Mosaic and Cashmere Stitches.)

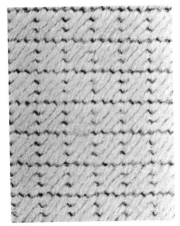

FIG. 11-8

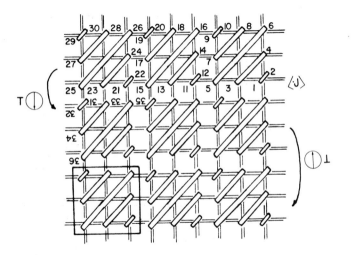

Giant scotch

FIG. 11-9

The Scotch Stitch can be worked in many sizes: 5-stitch, 7-stitch (a), 9-stitch (b), and 11-stitch (c). Keep in mind that the longer the stitches, the more likely they are to snag.

Use your thumb nail to move the first stitches aside so each newly laid stitch will lie flat on canvas and not on top of other stitches. (Take a Bargello Tuck, page 23.)

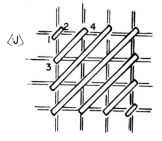

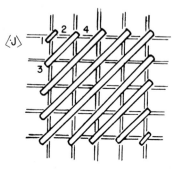

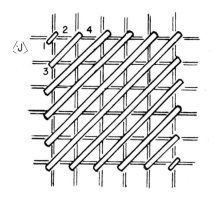

The tie is worked in the center of the longest stitch. This tie adds a bump and also reduces the likelihood of snagging.

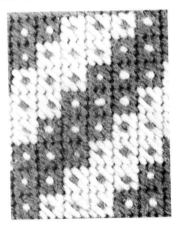

FIG. 11-10

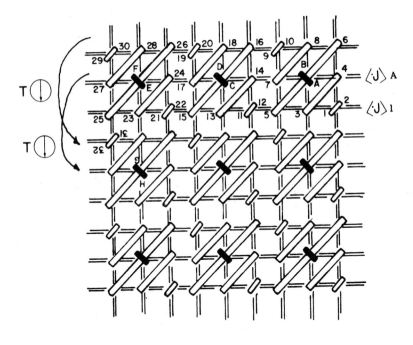

Framed scotch

Stitch the frame in the Continental Stitch. Work all the horizontal rows first. Work the vertical rows next, skipping the stitches that have been worked. Work a portion of vertical rows to ease turning the corner to the next row. Work missed areas as convenient.

FIG. 11-11

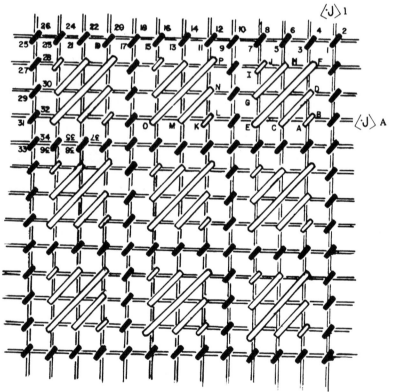

Try this stitch in one color. See Reversed Mosaic for hints on working Reserved Scotch.

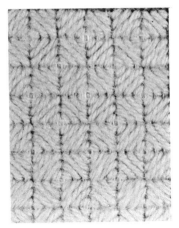

FIG. 11-12

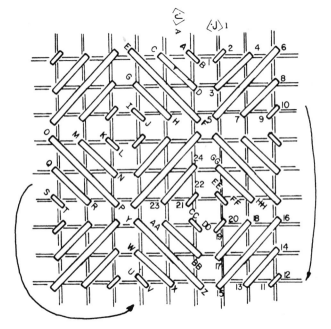

Chapter

Cross stitches

Cross Stitches make pretty filling, design, and border stitches. They often stand alone to represent flowers.

When worked on Regular Mono canvas, the Cross Stitch must be crossed as you go. Watch the numbering as you go through this section.

It does not matter whether you cross the right arm over the left or the left arm over the right—but you must be consistent. I find it easier to work the whole area in half of the cross first. Then I go back and cross those stitches. I manage to ruin it every time if I don't do this.

The Cross-Stitch sampler was worked on Penelope 7 canvas with Persian yarn. Many of the Cross Stitches did not need thickening; however, many did. When the Cross Stitch is worked on smaller canvas, it is not distinct. Larger Crosses can be worked successfully on smaller canvas.

CROSS STITCHES

	BORDER	GOOD BACKING	POOR BACKING	BACKGROUND	DESIGN	ACCENT	FAST	SLOW	GEOMETRIC PATTERN	YARN HOG	SNAGPROOF	LITTLE TEXTURE	MEDIUM TEXTURE	HIGH RELIEF	FLOWER STITCH	WEAK PATTERN	MEDIUM PATTERN	STRONG PATTERN	DISTORTS CANVAS
CROSS STITCH (see p. 194)				•	•			•	•	•	•	•			•	•			
RICE (see p. 195)	•				•	•		•	•			•			•			•	
2 x 2 CROSS (see p. 195)	•			•	•				•			•			•				
DOUBLE STITCH (see p. 196)				•	•				•				•				•		
UPRIGHT CROSS (see p. 196)				•	•				•	•	•	•				•			
SLASHED CROSS (see p. 197)				•	•	•			•	•			•		•	•			
SLANTED CROSS (see p. 197)	•			•	•				•			•				•			
BINDING STITCH (see p. 198)	•							•			•			•				•	
PLAITED GOBELIN (see p. 200)	•			•	•				•	•	•							•	
DOUBLE STRAIGHT CROSS (see p. 201)				•	•	•				•			•		•			•	
DOUBLE LEVIATHAN (see p. 202)	•				•	•			•		•				•	•	•		
TIED WINDMILL (see p. 203)						•			•	•			•					•	
SMYRNA CROSS (see p. 204)	•			•	•	•			•						•	•		•	

Cross stitch

FIG. 12-1

On Mono canvas, each Cross must be crossed right away. It is faster, however, to work Penelope or Interlock Mono with a Cross Stitch. Both look alike.

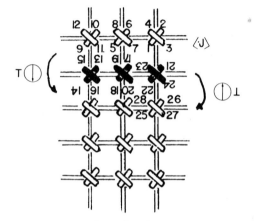

Cross Stitch:
Mono canvas

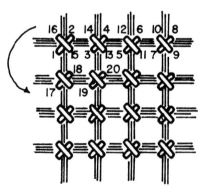

Cross Stitch:
Penelope canvas

Use this stitch for a border of varying widths.

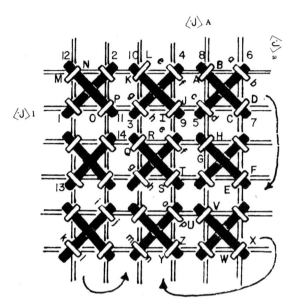

FIG. 12-2

2 × 2 cross

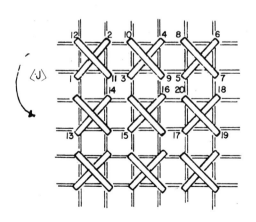

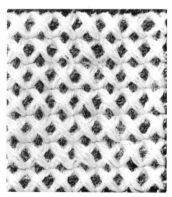

FIG. 12-3

Double stitch

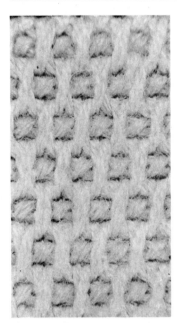

This is a good stitch for bumpy texture. When worked in one color, it resembles tree bark. It is also good for polka dots.

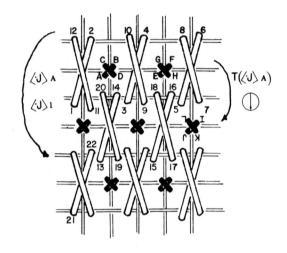

FIG. 12-4

Upright cross

FIG. 12-5

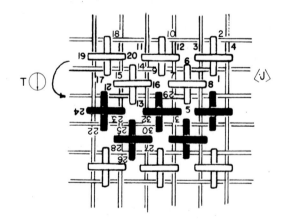

You will often have to use your finger to move the yarns to find where to place the difficult second row. It can stand alone.

FIG. 12-6

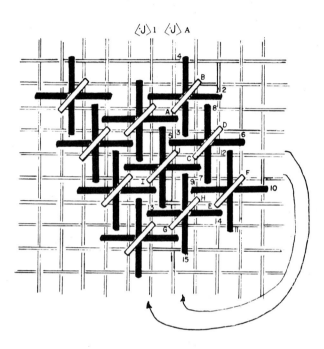

The first part of the stitch is the same as the Cross Stitch, but the return is like Straight Gobelin.

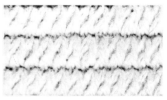

FIG. 12-7

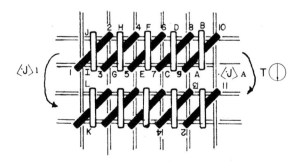

Binding stitch

The Binding Stitch is not only useful; it is attractive, too. It finishes edges and sews seams (page 61). It is worked only on the edge of the canvas. You will need 2 threads of the canvas to secure it properly. On Penelope this is 1 mesh; on Mono, 2 mesh.

It is worked much like the Fern Stitch, and it, too produces a braid. (Take a Bargello Tuck, page 23.)

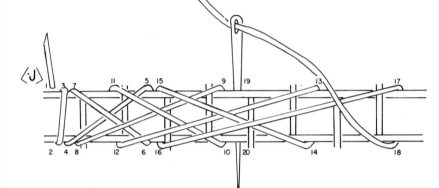

FIG. 12-8

Right

THE STITCHES

Wrong

FIG. 12-8 (continued)

Plaited gobelin

FIG. 12-9

Be sure your yarn will cover the canvas. Experiment. Use your thumb to push the yarn back to find the holes for the next stitch. Work from top to bottom only. Cut the yarn at the end of the first row, and begin the second row at the top. Do the compensating stitches last.

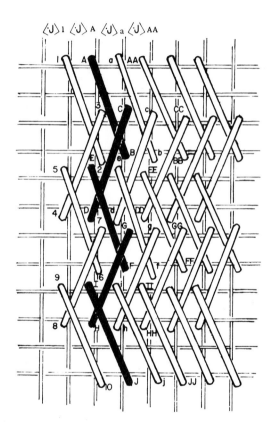

Double straight cross

FIG. 12-10

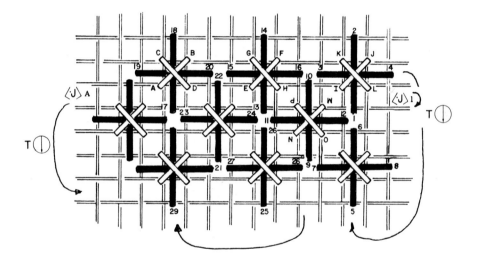

Double leviathan

FIG. 12-11

(Take a Bargello Tuck, page 23.)

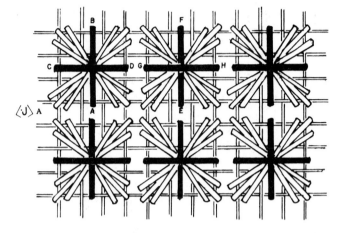

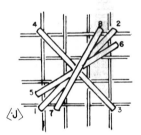

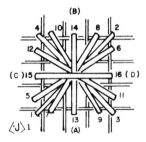

The Tied Windmill also stands alone. Put it on a ground of Cross Stitch if you wish.

FIG. 12-12

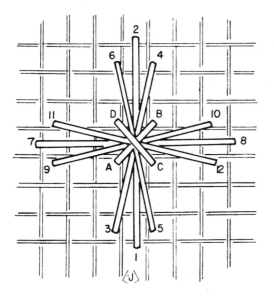

Smyrna cross

FIG. 12-13

Make the × first, then the +. Smyrna Cross makes a good bump. When the + is worked in a light color, the stitch resembles hot-cross buns. It is good for buttons, polka dots, etc.

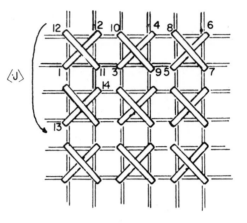

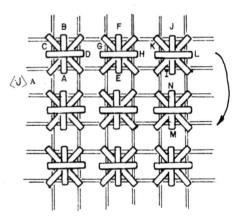

13

Tied, eye, and leaf stitches

TIED STITCHES

The Tied Stitches are pretty. These stitches are somewhat slow, but they mostly have good backings with little snagging on the right side of the canvas.

It is *most* important that you tie each stitch or group of stitches as you go. Each of the drawings is numbered: follow them closely. I recommend a Mono 12 or 14 for Tied Stitches.

TIED, EYE, AND LEAF STITCHES

Stitch	BORDER	GOOD BACKING	POOR BACKING	BACKGROUND	DESIGN	ACCENT	FAST	SLOW	GEOMETRIC PATTERN	SHADING	YARN HOG	SNAGS	SNAGPROOF	LITTLE TEXTURE	MEDIUM TEXTURE	HIGH RELIEF	FLOWER STITCH	WEAK PATTERN	MEDIUM PATTERN	STRONG PATTERN	DISTORTS CANVAS
KNOTTED STITCH (see p. 207)		●		●	●			●		●			●	●					●		
FLY (see p. 207)				●	●									●					●		
COUCHING (see p. 208)			●		●	●	●					●		●				●			
FRAMED STAR (see p. 210)	●	●			●	●			●	●		●				●	●		●		
DOUBLE STAR (see p. 211)	●	●			●	●			●	●						●	●		●		
DIAMOND RAY (see p. 212)		●		●	●	●			●	●						●	●		●		
RAY (see p. 213)	●	●				●			●	●	●					●	●		●		
LEAF #1 (see p. 214)	●	●		●	●	●			●	●		●		●					●		
ROUMANIAN LEAF (see p. 215)	●	●				●	●					●				●			●		
CLOSE HERRINGBONE (see p. 215)						●						●					●		●		
RAISED CLOSE HERRINGBONE (see p. 216)						●					●	●				●			●		

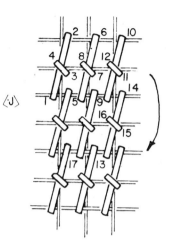

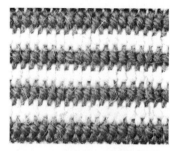

FIG. 13-1

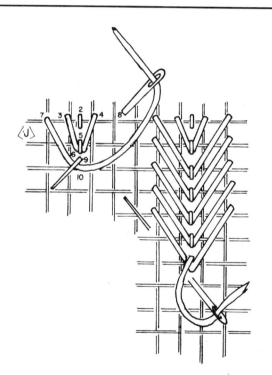

FIG. 13-2

Couching

Couching is laying one yarn where you want it and tacking it down with another yarn. It curves well. Thread two needles. Try to tie at even intervals.

FIG. 13-3

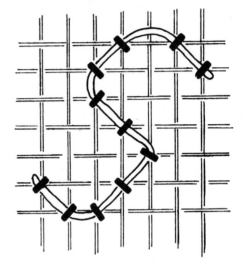

Eye stitches

Eye Stitches are those that are made by putting several stitches into one hole. This technique creates a hole, a dimple, or an eye.

Work Eye Stitches on Regular Mono 10. Use a full strand of tapestry or Persian yarn.

Eye Stitches are very pretty and interesting to do but slow to work up. In stitching them, work from the outside to the center, and *always* go *down* into the center. This will prevent splitting or snagging the yarn of the stitches you have already worked.

As you put what seems an impossible number of stitches into one small hole, take care that each of these stitches goes into the hole smoothly. If you are working on Regular Mono canvas, this task will be a little easier. It is a great help to enlarge the center hole by poking the point of a pair of embroidery scissors into it. Spread the mesh gently to enlarge the hole. This works *only* on Regular Mono canvas. Use two-ply Persian yarn on other kinds.

You may need to pull the yarn more tightly as each eye forms. This helps to make the stitch smooth, but be careful not to pull the canvas out of shape.

Note that Eye Stitches usually begin with an Upright Cross, going from the outside into the center. Next, one stitch is taken in each quadrant in a circular motion until all the remaining stitches have been taken. The even-numbered stitches are all in the center of the eye, and because they do not fit easily, the numbers have been omitted.

Eye Stitches lend themselves to broad borders, backgrounds, and pillows. Single motifs or clusters of two or three eyes make lovely flowers.

Because the Eye Stitches have good backing, most of them will wear well.

FIG. 13-4

Framed star

FIG. 13-5

Without the frame, this is simply the Star Stitch. The frame is necessary to cover the canvas, except on Mono 14.

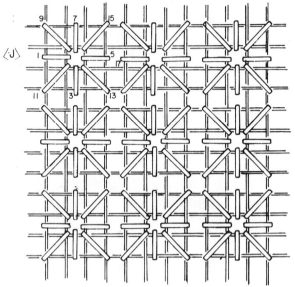

Star

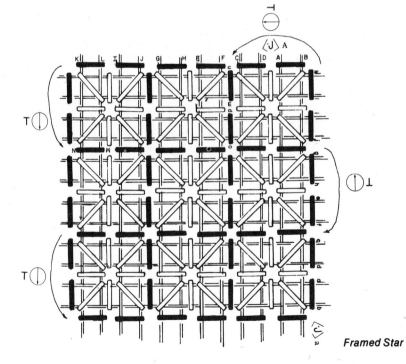

Framed Star

This stitch is actually a framed Reversed Mosaic. I think you will find it easier to get a smooth finish if you follow the numbers given. This stitch is particularly attractive in two colors.

FIG. 13-6

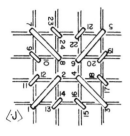

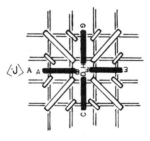

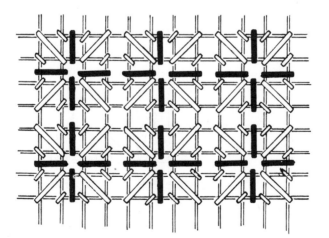

LEAF STITCHES

Leaf Stitches have a charm all their own; they complement lovely flowers. Given on the following pages are a few of those you can use. Mix them up, use one or two favorites, or make up your own.

Use the Leaf Stitches as overall patterns, singly, or in pairs. Turn Leaf Stitches sideways or upside down to make feathers. They may be worked in three ways:

1. from the top, one stitch to the right, one stitch to the left, etc.
2. from the bottom, one stitch to the right, one stitch to the left, etc.
3. from the bottom, up one side, and down the other. Work Leaf Stitches on Penelope or Mono 10. Usually a full strand of tapestry or Persian yarn covers.

Take a Bargello Tuck as you bury the tails (page 23).

Diamond ray

FIG. 13-7

The Diamond Ray Stitch makes a most interesting pattern and has a good backing. I generally like something faster to work up for a background, but you might want to use it that way. The longest stitch is not likely to snag.

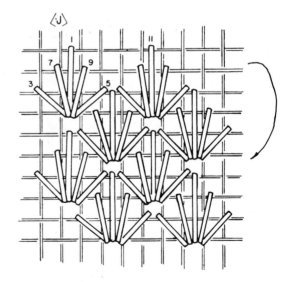

The Ray Stitch is also very slow to work up and is hard on the fingers. Try spreading the base hole with a pair of scissors as described on pages 208–9. In spite of its drawbacks, this stitch is worthwhile, for it is lovely when finished. It makes a good bumpy border but is not recommended for large areas.

FIG. 13-8

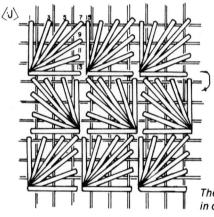

These Ray Stitches are worked in one color

Leaf #1

FIG. 13-9

This is the basic and most familiar Leaf Stitch. It makes an interesting pattern. It is lovely when shaded within each leaf. An optional vein may be added. This had a good backing and makes a pretty border or vertical stripe.

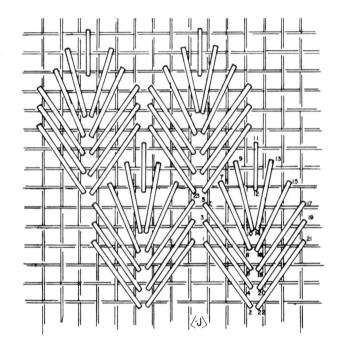

The Roumanian-type stitches (Roumanian Leaf and Fly Stitch) are fast and fun to work. Refer to the Fly Stitch; page 207. Shading within the leaf can be done, but then the speed of the stitch is lost.

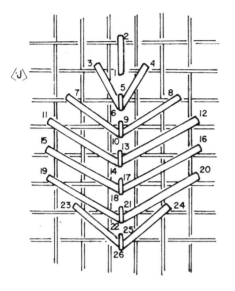

FIG. 13-10

Close herringbone

This makes a slightly raised leaf, made by crossing stitches over each other. There is some backing but not a great deal. This stitch stands alone and makes a long, smooth leaf.

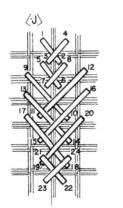

FIG. 13-11

Raised close herringbone

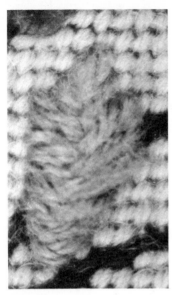

FIG. 13-12

This leaf is quite three-dimensional and is interesting to work. It is worked in steps that produce a fair backing. Again, this Leaf Stitch is used alone as an accent for a design. The needle penetrates the canvas only at the tip of the leaf and as it is worked to the rear. Only the first stitch at the base goes through the canvas. The rest of the stitches go under the first stitch on top of the canvas. The size and shape can be readily varied.

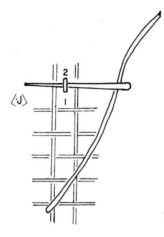

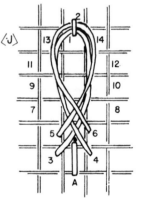

Chapter 14

Decorative stitches

These decorative stitches have many uses, some quite specialized and some more broad. They are not related in construction technique.

DECORATIVE STITCHES

	BORDER	GOOD BACKING	POOR BACKING	BACKGROUND	DESIGN	ACCENT	FAST	SLOW	GEOMETRIC PATTERN	SHADING	YARN HOG	SNAGS	SNAGPROOF	LITTLE TEXTURE	MEDIUM TEXTURE	HIGH RELIEF	FLOWER STITCH	WEAK PATTERN	MEDIUM PATTERN	STRONG PATTERN	DISTORTS CANVAS
BUTTONHOLE (see p. 219)	•		•		•	•			•			•		•				•			
BUTTONHOLE IN HALF-CIRCLE (see p. 220)				•	•	•			•	•		•			•					•	
CHAIN (see p. 221)	•		•		•	•								•						•	
WOVEN SPIDER WEB (see p. 223)			•			•		•			•					•	•			•	
SMOOTH SPIDER WEB (see p. 223)			•			•		•			•					•	•			•	
RIDGED SPIDER WEB (see p. 224)			•			•		•			•					•	•			•	
WOUND CROSS (see p. 224)			•			•		•			•					•	•			•	
FRENCH KNOT (see p. 225)			•			•		•				•		•			•		•		
FRENCH KNOTS ON STALKS (see p. 226)			•			•		•				•		•			•		•		
BULLION KNOT (see p. 227)			•			•		•			•	•				•	•			•	
STARFISH (see p. 228)					•	•								•						•	
THORN (see p. 228)			•			•		•				•		•						•	
LOOPED TURKEY WORK (see p. 229)			•	•	•	•				•	•	•				•	•		•		
CUT TURKEY WORK (see p. 230)			•	•	•	•				•	•	•				•	•	•			
LAZY DAISY (see p. 231)			•		•	•						•		•			•		•		
NEEDLEWEAVING (see p. 231)			•		•	•						•			•		•			•	
RAISED CUP STITCH (see p. 232)			•			•			•		•	•				•	•			•	
RAISED ROPE (see p. 233)			•		•	•						•				•	•		•		
RAISED BUTTONHOLE (see p. 234)			•		•			•		•						•			•		
RAISED BUTTONHOLE ON RAISED BAND (see p. 235)			•		•				•	•	•					•					
SHISHA (see p. 235)			•			•			•							•	•			•	

Buttonhole

The Buttonhole Stitch has many variations. Two are given here.

  This stitch creates a smooth area and a ridge. Arrange these areas to suit your purposes. Disregard the mesh. Treat the canvas as if it were fabric, and stitch. When worked as shown here, horizontal stripes are created.

  Work the rows from bottom to top and from left to right. To change from one strand of yarn to the next, you will need two needles threaded with the same color yarn. If, for example, your yarn runs out at #8 on the drawing, insert the needle into the canvas at #8, leaving the yarn from #7 to #8 a little loose. Let this needle dangle on the wrong side of the canvas. Bury the tail of the yarn on the second needle on the wrong side. Bring the needle up at #9. Let this second needle dangle. Adjust the tension on the first needle, and bury the tail. Continue with the second needle.

FIG. 14-1

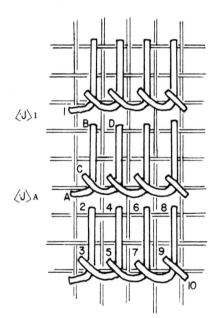

Buttonhole in half-circle

This stitch makes a lovely filler for a field or faraway flower garden. Make sure that the stitches that go into the middle are even (see Eye Stitches, page 208).

FIG. 14-2

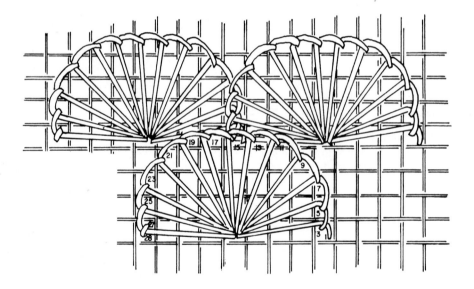

The Chain Stitch is quite a versatile stitch. It is one of a few stitches that curves. You may work it on top of the background or leave a space in the background to work the Chain Stitch.

This stitch is easier to work if you turn the canvas so that you are working horizontally and from right to left.

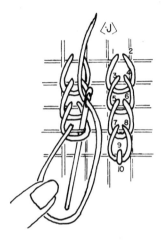

FIG. 14-3

Spider webs

There are some instructions for working Spider Webs that are basic to all three versions.

Lay one of the foundations shown in the figure below. Only the Woven Spider Web *must* have an odd number of spokes. If these spokes are not *well secured,* the whole thing will come undone. Take a Bargello Tuck (page 23).

Bring the needle up as close to the center as you can without actually coming through the center. Work this yarn in the pattern of the stitch you are doing. Do not penetrate the canvas until you are through. Keep going around and around until the spokes are no longer visible. When you think you cannot possibly get one more round in, do two more—then you are through.

To make a high ball, pull the yarn tightly but not so tightly that the spokes become misshapen. As you take each stitch, pull the yarn toward the center. This helps to tighten the stitch.

You may change colors or techniques midstream. For example, you can make a wheel by working Woven Spider Web (for the hub), Ridged Spider Web (for the spokes), and Smooth Spider Web (for the rim).

Use Spider Webs for grapes, apples, other fruit, wheels, balls, buttons, flowers, ladybugs, spiders, and other insects—anything round.

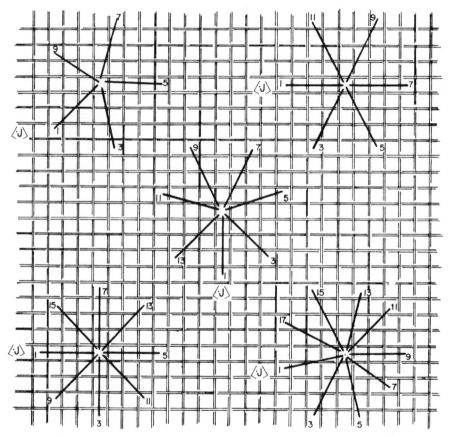

FIG. 14-4 *Spider Web Foundations.*

Woven spider web

Lay the spokes. You must have an odd number. Weave the yarn over and under the spokes. When you think you cannot possibly get one more row in, do two more. Then you are through.

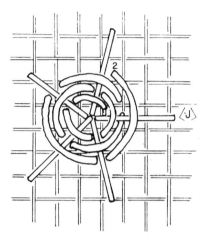

FIG. 14-5

Smooth spider web

Go over two spokes and back under one; over two, under one; etc.

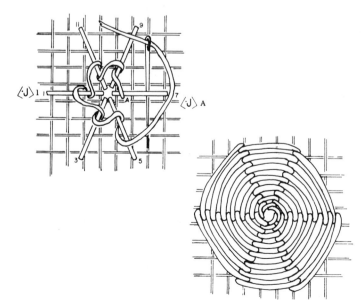

FIG. 14-6

Ridged spider web

FIG. 14-7

Reverse the process of the preceding stitch. Go under two spokes and back over one; under two, over one.

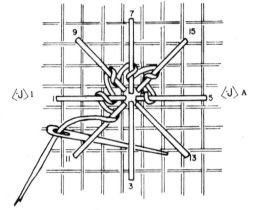

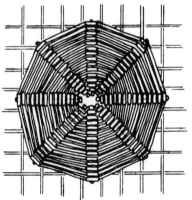

Wound cross

FIG. 14-8

This is another good round stitch. Make it as fat as you like. Wind the yarn under all the spokes without penetrating the canvas.

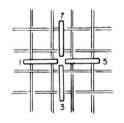

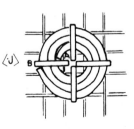

French Knots are handy. They fill bare canvas, make polka dots, flower centers, whole flowers, etc.

FIG. 14-9

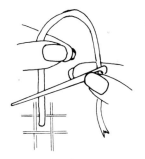

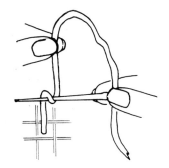

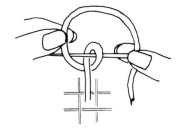

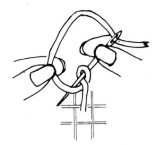

French knots on stalks

FIG. 14-10

These are an expanded version of the French Knot. They make lovely flowers and good insect antennae.

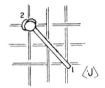

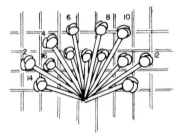

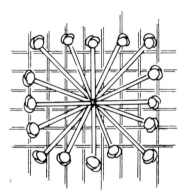

The Bullion Knot is worked by laying a thread and wrapping a yarn around it—without penetrating the canvas. Be sure that the tail is well secured. Pull tightly; and it will curl. Worked loosely, this stitch resembles finger curls.

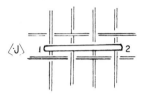

FIG. 14-11

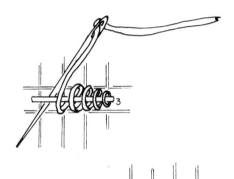

Starfish

FIG. 14-12

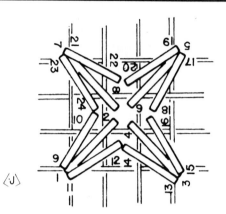

Thorn

FIG. 14-13

This stitch is good for making ferns and stems with small leaves or thorns. Curve it to suit your purposes.

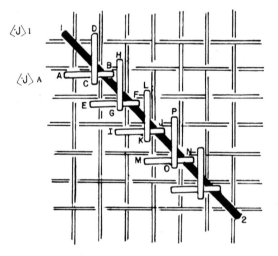

Stitch the *bottom* row first, and work *up*. Work from left to right only. This means that you must cut your yarn at the end of every row. There is no tail to bury; it becomes part of the stitch. You may skip rows on a small canvas if it is too crowded.

Use a strip of paper to help you get the loops even (see following page). In working Looped Turkey Work, try not to run out of yarn in the middle of a row unless you have to.

Turkey Work should be worked on an even number of mesh. However, when you get to the end of a row, there often is a mesh left over. Work the last 3 mesh by leaving the extra 1 in the center of the stitch. (You are actually skipping a mesh.)

Work your whole design first; then put this stitch in. If you do not, you will never be able to move this stitch aside to get the others in.

FIG. 14-14

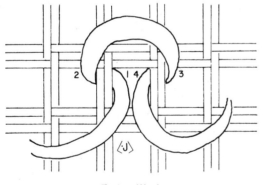

Turkey Work

Looped Turkey Work

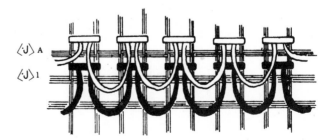

Cut turkey work

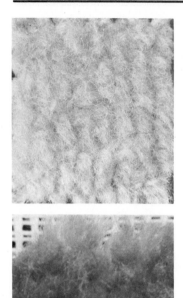

FIG. 14-15

Work just as in Looped Turkey Work, but cut the loops as you go. After working Row 2, clip Row 1; after working Row 3, clip Row 2. If you cut each row immediately after it is worked, the pieces can be easily caught in the next row as you stitch it. However, if you wait until you have completely finished the area, it is quite hard to do a good cutting job. Cut as shown below.

Cutting the loops too short causes the rows to show. See top photo (right) and bottom photo (wrong). It does not matter if you end a yarn in the middle of a row. Persian yarn makes a fluffier Cut Turkey Work.

Work your whole design first; then put this stitch in. If you do not, you won't be able to move this stitch aside to get the others in.

To fluff your Turkey Work, pick at it with the point of the needle. Trim carefully.

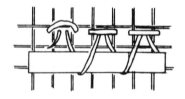

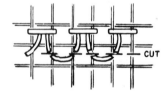

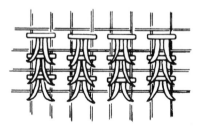

Lazy daisy

Work this stitch on top of a background stitch. It can serve as flower petals, leaves, and many other things.

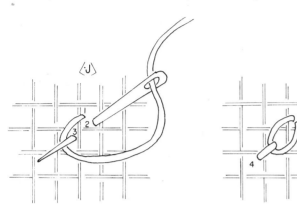

FIG. 14-16

Needleweaving

This is a kind of surface embroidery. The yarn penetrates the canvas only at the outer edges of the area covered in Needleweaving. Any pattern and/or number of spokes you wish may be woven.

FIG. 14-17

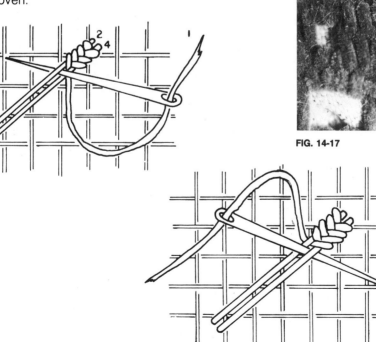

Raised cup stitch

FIG. 14-18

Make a triangle of yarn as illustrated. This is the last time your needle will go through the canvas. Slide the needle under one side of the triangle, without going through the canvas (see below). Put the needle under and then over the thread on the needle as illustrated. Pull the needle through and tug gently, making a somewhat loose knot (see below).

Do this again on the same side of the triangle. Keep going around the triangle, making two knots on each side. Note that each of these knots is connected with a short piece of yarn. (See arrow in drawing below.) It is on this bar that you will secure the second row of knots. Make one knot on each bar as you go around the second time. Keep going around until the cup is as big as you would like it to be. Adding one knot on each bar merely makes the cup higher. You will have to place two or three on each bar as you go around if you wish to increase the diameter of the cup.

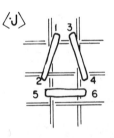

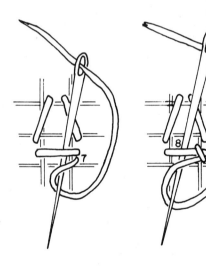

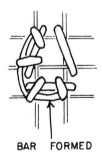

BAR FORMED

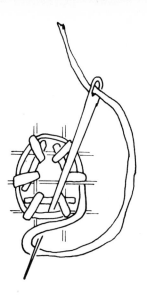

FIG. 14-18 (continued)

Raised rope

Work the stitches very loosely. They will automatically form a ridge. Curve the stitch as you need to. This stitch works particularly well in a circle. It may also be worked side by side to fill an area.

FIG. 14-19

Decorative stitches

233

Raised buttonhole

Always work this stitch from left to right. Work the vertical rows of this stitch from top to bottom. Work the rows from left to right for a compact stitch, and work them from right to left for a lacy look.

When working the buttonhole portion of the stitch from left to right, pull the thread with your left hand, keeping it taut until the next stitch is taken. Use your fingernail or the points of small scissors to push the vertical rows together. This helps to pack the yarn in for height.

This stitch makes nice tree bark.

FIG. 14-20

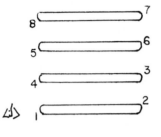

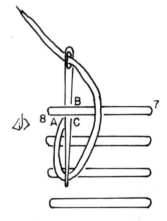

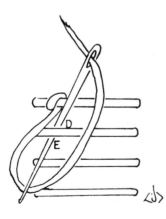

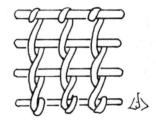

Raised buttonhole on raised band

This is the same stitch as the preceding one except for the bed over which the stitch is worked. The fatter the padding you lay down, the higher the stitch will be. Lay as many stitches as you need. Build up the center for a rounded look. Stagger the start and stop of padding stitches to get a smooth, long look. After you have laid the padding, refer to Raised Buttonhole to continue working the stitch.

This stitch is *very hard* to rip, so be sure that is what you want to do before you put it in.

This stitch makes particularly nice tree bark.

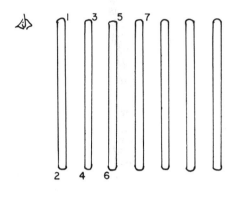

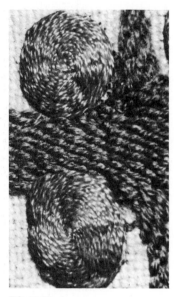

FIG. 14-21

Shisha

This stitch is good for attaching such things to canvas as mirrors and gems. It does better with flat things, but items with some height or thickness may be attached with it.

Stitches #1 to #16 form holding threads. Steps A–H begin the processes of covering the holding threads with decorative stitches. Continue the steps as shown in F & G all the way around the circle.

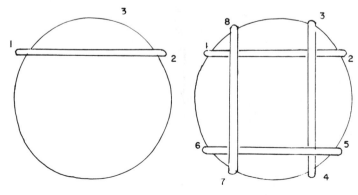

FIG. 14-22

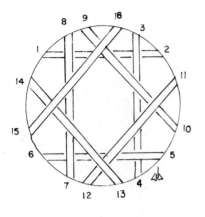

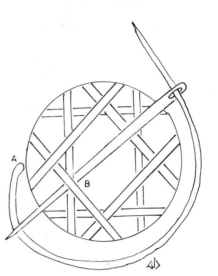

FIG. 14-22 (continued)

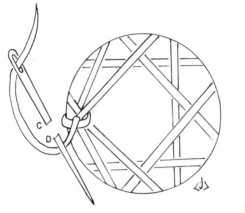

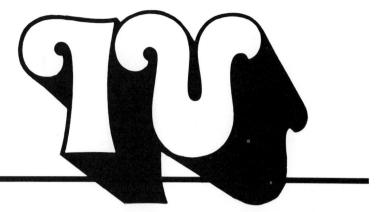

BLOCKING AND FINISHING

Good finishing is essential to any piece of needlepoint. Professional-looking finishing enhances perfect stitching and causes sloppy stitching to be overlooked.

You can achieve this at home. Follow the directions given in this chapter step by step. Don't go on to the next step if the first step isn't right.

So many people think the job's done when the last stitch is taken. Not so—the most critical part is left: the finishing. It is the finishing that gives the viewer of your project that vital first impression. Your stitching will be noticed only upon close inspection.

Blocking, the first step of professional finishing, is clearly described in Chapter 15. The making of pillows and linings, the mounting of needle-point pictures, and other finishing techniques are outlined in Chapter 16.

Chapter **15**

Blocking

B locking is the first step to professional finishing. If you farm it out, professional blockers will charge you an arm and a leg. Doing it yourself is cheaper. Besides, if you're a perfectionist, very few people will do it to your satisfaction. Pieces worked on plastic canvas do not need to be blocked.

So roll up your sleeves, and put a little elbow grease into your needlepoint.

Blocking board

First you'll need a blocking board. I like to use insulation board (without the tar). There seem to be many names for it, but the men at the lumberyard always know what I'm talking about when I tell them it's the stuff people make bulletin boards out of. Sometimes they'll give you a scrap, in which case you, of course, will not be picky about the size or shape. (Isn't it amazing how adaptable we can be when the price is right?) If they have to cut a 4′ × 8′ sheet for you, 2′ × 2′ is a handy size to have and use.

I like the insulation board because it is porous, and

needlepoint dries on it more quickly than it does on plywood. Also, pins and staples go into and pull out of it easily.

Cover the board. The color of the board rubs off easily, and the roughness of it will snag your needlepoint. Staple a brown paper bag to both sides of the board. Bind the edges with masking tape, covering the staples. A cheap paper bag works better than brown wrapping paper. It's OK to piece it if you have to.

Right before you go to bed, put the board in the bathtub. Wet the paper thoroughly with water. Then go to bed! It will look so awful that you'll be sure you've done something wrong. (You haven't!) The next morning, the paper will be dry, smooth and beautifully taut!

Making the grid

Blocking will be easier if you have a grid pattern drawn on the paper. The lines must be *perpendicular* and *parallel*. One-inch squares are handy to use, but lines the width of the yardstick are easier to make. Draw the lines on with a *waterproof* marker. Test it yourself (page 14). When the ink has dried completely, spray your board with a spray plastic (acrylic). Mine has lasted five years so far.

Gingham makes a prettier board cover but it's not any easier to get the gingham lines straight than it is to draw lines parallel and perpendicular. You still need to cover the board with paper, because the insulation board will stain the fabric and, perhaps, your needlepoint. (Heaven forbid!) Use only *woven* gingham fabric. You can tell it from printed gingham because the woven gingham looks the same on both sides. One-hundred-percent cotton is best; but if you must use a blend, the more cotton there is, the better it will work. One-inch squares will be easiest to stretch over the board, but ¼" or ½" squares will make blocking easier. You will be able to see black (or navy) and white squares more readily than other colors. Do *NOT* preshrink the fabric.

Stretch the fabric over the board so it is taut. Staple it in place. If it's not taut, you could catch a tuck in blocking your needlepoint piece. This would throw the lines off, and the needlepoint would then be crooked.

Put the board in the bathtub again. Pour very hot water over the fabric, letting the excess run off. One-hundred-percent cotton will shrink. Some permanent press fabrics will not shrink enough, but most will.

Before you start stitching, measure the area to be stitched. Write the measurements on the masking tape that you've used to bind the raw edges of the canvas. Use a *waterproof* marker, of course! This is the size your needlepoint should be blocked to.

Follow the instructions in Figure 15-1a–j for blocking. Pieces stitched with texture should be blocked face up.

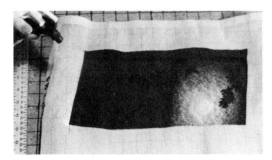

FIG. 15-1a *Wet your needlepoint with a spray of water.*

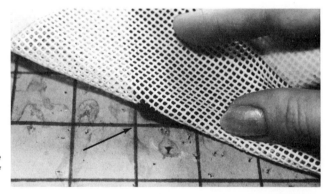

FIG. 15-1b *Put one corner of the needlepoint at the intersection of two lines on the blocking board.*

FIG. 15-1c *Staple this corner in place with three or four staples. They will be under lots of tension later.*

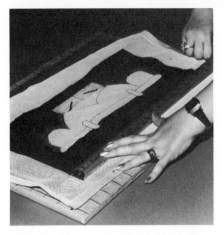

FIG. 15-1d *Measure along one side as shown in Figure 15-3b, and staple the second corner. Measure between the second and third corner; staple the third corner. Then staple between the three corners.*

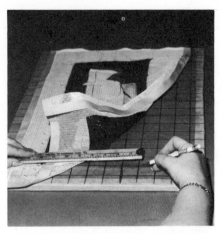

FIG. 15-1e *Find the point for the fourth corner by measuring. Mark this point on the blocking board.*

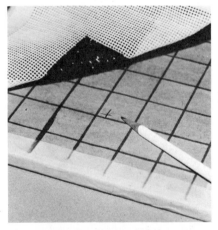

FIG. 15-1f *Your mark should look like this.*

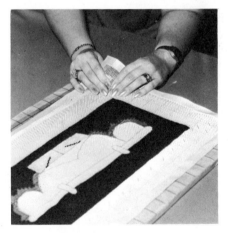

FIG. 15-1g *Pull the fourth corner to meet your mark. If your needlepoint is badly out of shape, you'll need one to three people to help you at this point. Staple the corner in place securely.*

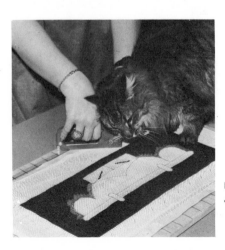

FIG. 15-1h *Is feline help better than no help at all?*

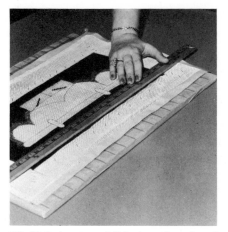

FIG. 15-1i *Lay a yardstick along the edge of the needlepoint to help you get the side straight.*

FIG. 15-1j *Staple the corners down so they'll dry flat.*

Fastening the canvas

Use a staple gun to block when you have a substantial margin of blank canvas around your stitching. The staple gun may break a few mesh. But if you're worried about it, put the staples out a couple of inches from the stitching. Put the staples about ¼" apart and at an angle to the mesh. This gives the staples the best grip on the canvas.

If you've used the Two-Step Edge-Finishing Method, you won't have this blank canvas to staple onto. Use heavy-duty *stainless steel* T-pins. Put them between the stitches and two to three stitches in from the edge—very carefully. They, too, should be ¼" apart. Blocking crushes the Binding Stitch, so the Binding Stitch should be done *after* blocking.

The T-pins leave holes in the needlepoint. Push the yarn back in place with a needle and a *little* steam. NEVER TOUCH THE IRON TO THE NEEDLEPOINT.

The needlepoint should be completely dry before you take it off the blocking board. It may take as little as 24–48 hours or as long as a week to dry. If you take the needlepoint off the blocking board while it is wet, it will, most likely, revert to its former crooked life.

NEVER prop up the blocking board. Your needlepoint may dry with a watermark if you do. Watermarks do *not* come out. Keep the board flat until the needlepoint dries. Uneven dampening also causes watermarks.

Stains

If your yarn, paint, or marker runs during blocking, a couple of things can be tried before you have to resort to ripping. Don't let the needlepoint dry, by any means. Sponge the stain with a mixture of 1 teaspoon of ammonia and 1 cup of water. Rinse thoroughly.

If that doesn't work, soak the piece in cold water overnight. If that doesn't work, block it and let it dry. Then the only alternative is to rip the discolored stitches and work them again. (Sorry!) But remember—Blessed is a cheerful ripper!

Hints

Raised stitches can be fluffed with a shot of steam. Do *NOT* overdo. Too much steam shrinks and mats the wool.

A limp piece of needlepoint can be revived with spray starch on the wrong side.

Correcting distortion

Sometimes no matter how carefully you have blocked, a needlepoint piece will pop out of shape again. This is particularly true of large-mesh canvases (3½, 4, 5, and 7) and of stitches that distort (see the charts at the beginning of each stitch chapter).

Pieces that are only a little bit out of shape can be kept on the straight and narrow with an iron-on interfacing (available in fabric stores). You cannot do this with Raised Stitches, however.

Badly distorted pieces will need rabbit-skin glue. You can buy it in art supply stores. Rabbit-skin glue comes in a powdered form, and it must be cooked. It will gel several hours later. Follow the instructions that come with it.

It should be put on the wrong side of the needlepoint. Pieces that have flat stitches are blocked face down. Put the rabbit-skin glue on while the piece is still on the blocking board. Put it on *thinly*.

Block the Raised-Stitch pieces as described above. While it's drying, make a frame from strips of soft wood (1" × 2"). It needs to be larger than the finished area of needlepoint (Figure 15-2a). Staple the margin of blank canvas to the frame. Then apply the rabbit-skin glue *thinly,* and allow it to dry thoroughly.

If there is no margin of blank canvas, you'll need to make the inside dimensions of the frame ¼" smaller on each side than the needlepoint. So if your piece is 8" x 10", the inside edges of the frame should be 7½" x 9½". Cover the wood of the frame with masking tape to protect your needlepoint.

The soft wood lets you use T-pins to attach the needlepoint to the frame. You may also use rustproof tacks and a hammer. The thickness of the wood lifts the Raised Stitches off the surface of the table. See Figure 15-2b & c. Allow it to dry overnight.

I cannot recommend rabbit-skin glue for rugs, however. One woman's dog ate her rug! (True!) Use liquid latex for rugs.

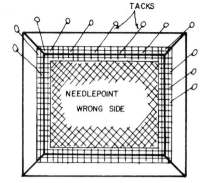

FIG. 15-2a *Frame for applying rabbit-skin glue.*

FIG. 15-2b *Materials used for applying rabbit-skin glue.*

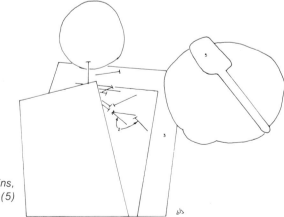

FIG. 15-2c *(1) canvas, (2) T-pins, (3) frame, (4) mixing bowl, (5) spatula.*

FIG. 15-2d–f
Applying rabbit-skin glue.

FIG. 15-2d

FIG. 15-2e

FIG. 15-2f

BLOCKING AND FINISHING

Chapter **16**

Finishing

This is yet another plateau at which people draw the line on how far the making of a project goes. Even I succumb to an *expert* finisher if the price is right. The upholsterer who finishes pillows in my area does a wonderful job, and he does it so cheaply that it's not worth the time and effort to do it myself.

But for the most part, I don't trust anyone to do finishing for me. Usually no one can do a good enough job to please me, and—on top of it all—I'm usually charged so much for the shoddy service that I can't see paying it. Do you agree? Then read on.

Framing

Needlepoint pictures can cost a bundle to finish. But if you plan ahead, you can cut the cost drastically by designing your project so that it fits into a standard-sized frame.

Some of these frames come already put together, and others come in strips. These are easy to assemble yourself. Check out the sizes available *before* you cut the canvas.

Once in a while, I'm forced to get a custom frame made. But I still mount the needlepoint myself. This way I save some money—but more important, I'm sure the needlepoint is mounted straight. (You see, I'm picky!)

The frame you select should be deep enough to cover a stretcher frame. The stretcher frame should not stick out beyond the back of your decorative frame. If it does, you'll need to stretch your needlepoint over a piece of ¼" plywood instead of a stretcher frame. *Never* use cardboard for this job. It buckles under the tension put on it. Humidity also causes the cardboard to buckle. Stretcher strips can be bought in art supply stores.

NEVER put needlepoint under glass. The wool needs air to breathe.

There is a trick to getting your needlepoint to fit a frame of a predetermined size. You *must* measure carefully. Always allow a 3" margin of blank canvas all the way around your design. For example, if your needlepoint design area is 5" × 7", then you need to cut the canvas 11" × 13". This was figured this way: 3" + 5" + 3" = 11" and 3" + 7" + 3" = 13". See Figure 16-1a for another example.

This may seem like a lot of wasted canvas to you, but it's not really. In blocking, you should pull only on blank canvas, not on the stitched area. Also, framing eats up much of this margin.

Mark the margins with a *waterproof* marker. It should be

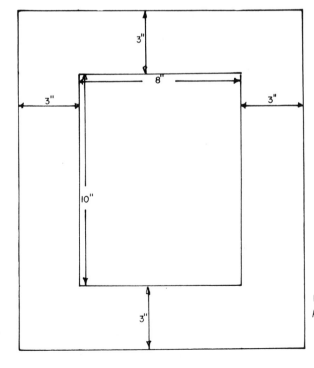

FIG. 16-1a *Measuring for needlepoint picture.*

marked 2 mesh shy (1 on either side) of your measurement. See Figure 16-1b. Actually, what you're doing is leaving a blank mesh all the way around your design. This is your fudge factor. Use a ruler when you block to maintain the *exact* same measurement.

See Figure 16-2a–o for instructions on framing.

A velvet liner is a nice elegant touch to finish needlepoint. Ask your framer about it.

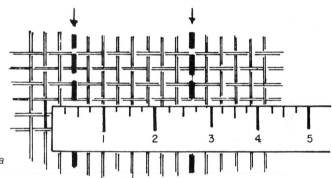

FIG. 16-1b *Measuring margins for a 3" picture.*

FIG. 16-2a *Equipment needed for framing needlepoint.*

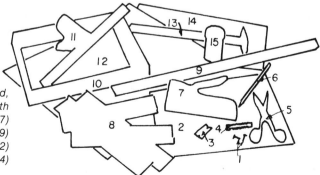

FIG. 16-2b *(1) tacks, (2) cardboard, (3) razor blade, (4) sawtooth hanger, (5) scissors, (6) pencil, (7) staple gun, (8) stretcher frame, (9) ruler, (10) frame, (11) square, (12) needlepoint, (13) hammer, (14) paper bag, (15) glue.*

FIG. 16-2c *Stretcher-frame pieces fit together at the corners like this; they may need a tap of the hammer to get them all the way together.*

FIG. 16-2d *Use a square to be sure each corner is 90°.*

FIG. 16-2e *Try stretcher frame in frame for size; note that there is very little extra room.*

FIG. 16-2f *Cut piece of cardboard a little smaller than stretcher frame, and staple it in place on stretcher frame; wrap needlepoint around stretcher frame so that cardboard lies next to needlepoint.*

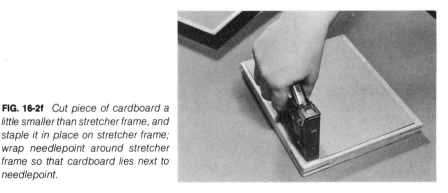

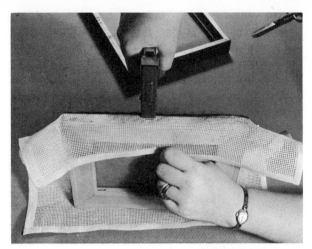

FIG. 16-2g *Staple corners first, then sides.*

FIG. 16-2h *When all sides are stapled, miter corners on back; staple middle of piece brought to wrong side of stretcher frame first.*

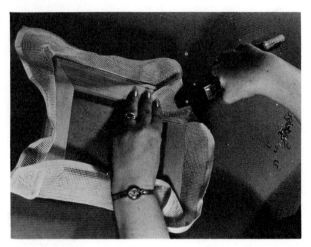

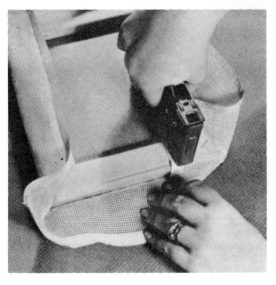

FIG. 16-2i (left) *Next staple sides of that same piece.*

FIG. 16-2j (below) *Fold one side of canvas to back to form one-half of mitered corner; then fold other side back and staple; do other three corners; then staple sides between mitered corners.*

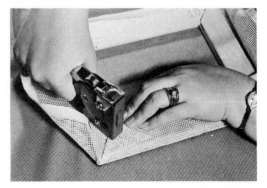

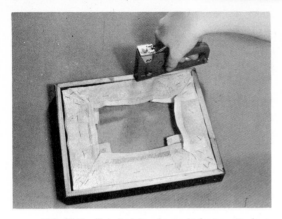

FIG. 16-2k *Put stretcher frame in frame; staple or nail stretcher frame in place.*

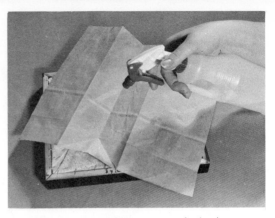

FIG. 16-2l *Wet piece of brown paper for back.*

FIG. 16-2m *Apply Elmer's Glue-All to back of frame, and wipe away excess glue with damp paper towel.*

FIG. 16-2n *Place paper over back of picture frame, and trim away excess paper with single-edged razor blade; again wipe away excess glue.*

FIG. 16-2o *Find center of picture and attach sawtooth hanger; the paper will dry out, and you will have a picture that looks better than a professional could make it.*

The Intertwined Rainbows (page 91), the House (page 101), and Northwest Autumn (page 147) need special tricks for getting a decorative frame to cover the working frame. A piece of wood should be built so that it will cover the sides of the working frame. The top edges can be finished with a piece of molding like that used for trim in houses.

Pillows

Pillows are a popular needlepoint item, but they, too, can be very expensive to have finished professionally. If you sew at all, you can do your own!

Choose a suitable backing fabric. You might consider Ultra Suede (a synthetic), upholsterer's velvet, cotton suede, or no-wale corduroy.

Insert

By inserting a small piece of needlepoint into a piece of fabric, you can create an attractive pillow. The actual insertion of the needlepoint must be done by hand stitching it to the fabric.

Measure your needlepoint very carefully. Mark the size of the needlepoint on the wrong side of the fabric with tailor's chalk. Measure in ⅝" from that line, and mark another line. This will be your cutting line (see Figure 16-3). Cut on the solid line shown in the figure. Slash the corners *almost* to the dotted line.

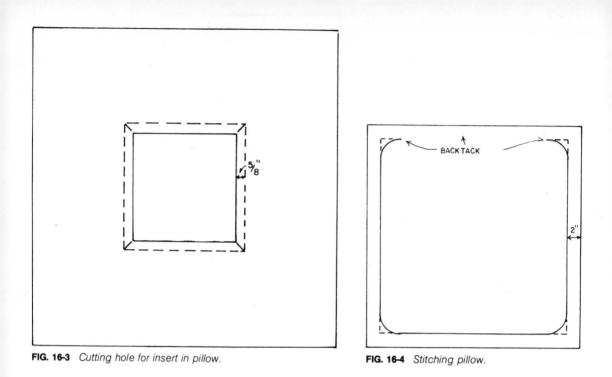

FIG. 16-3 *Cutting hole for insert in pillow.*

FIG. 16-4 *Stitching pillow.*

Put the needlepoint on a table, right side up. Put the fabric (also right side up) on top of the needlepoint. Tuck in the seam allowances, and pin the fabric to the needlepoint. Use the Blind Stitch (Figure 16-5) to secure it. Be sure you cover the canvas.

Finish the hand-stitched seam with a Twisted Cord (page 255).

Pillow construction

To make the needlepoint (inserted into a piece of fabric) and the fabric backing into a pillow, place the right sides together, and stitch as shown in Figure 16-4. Round the corners slightly.

Trim the seams to ⅝". Zigzag the raw edges together except at the opening; do those separately.

Turn and stuff with polyester fiber filling. Don't skimp on the corners. The pillow should be plump but not fat. A too-fat pillow will wrinkle on the sides.

Pin the opening together. Sew it with the Blind Stitch (Figure 16-5). Run the needle inside the fold of the fabric. Bring it out to catch one thread of the canvas. Insert it into the fabric again, and repeat the instructions. Take stitches every ¼" to ⅜".

BLOCKING AND FINISHING

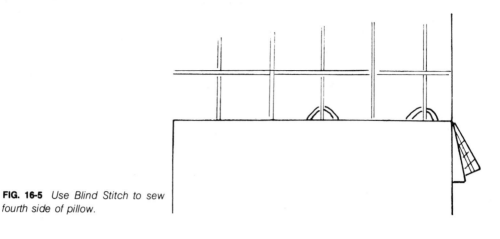

FIG. 16-5 *Use Blind Stitch to sew fourth side of pillow.*

Twisted cord

Unless you are an experienced seamstress, I do not recommend that you insert fabric cording into the seam of a pillow. A Twisted Cord is easier to make, and I think it's prettier.

You'll need a friend to help you make a Twisted Cord. First measure the distance around your pillow (or whatever). Multiply this number by 3. The result is the length of yarn you'll need to make a Twisted Cord long enough to go all the way around your pillow. Let's say your pillow is 14″ x 14″. The circumference is, then, 56″; so 56″ x 3 = 168″.

The thickness of your cord depends on how many strands you use. Six strands of yarn make a good thickness for a pillow cording. Two or three strands would be better to trim the opening on an insert. You will need, obviously, an uncut skein of yarn for this.

Knot the strands together at each end. Also knot them together in the middle. Attach one end to one beater of an electric mixer with a bread twist tie. Have your friend hold the

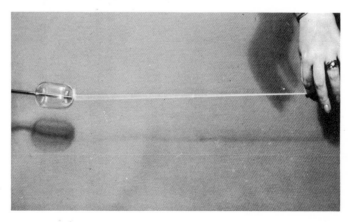

FIG. 16-6a–d
Making a Twisted Cord.

FIG. 16-6a

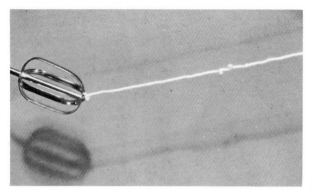

FIG. 16-6b

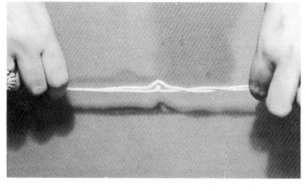

FIG. 16-6c

FIG. 16-6d

other end. Hold the yarn taut. Turn the mixer on, and run it until the yarn kinks. Keeping the yarn *taut,* hook the middle knot over a hook (or a third person's finger). Release your end from the mixer, and give it to the friend who's holding the other end of yarn. Take the yarn off the hook, and *slowly* release the tension. The two sections of yarn will now twist together (see Figure 16-6). Don't let go too fast; the twist will be sloppy. Tie the ends together with another piece of yarn so they won't untwist. Hand sew it in place. Don't let your stitches show. Tuck the ends in, and minimize the lump as best you can.

Linings

Use a lightweight lining fabric. Turn a ⅝" seam allowance under. Sew the lining in place with the Blind Stitch (page 255). If the needlepoint is to be folded (as on the Scissors Case), line it while it is flat. Cut the lining into two separate pieces, and sew them in place, leaving a space of ¼" to ⅜" on the fold line. This minimizes bulk at the fold. Then fold and continue finishing.

Jody's needlepoint box

Carefully trim the canvas so that there will be a margin of blank canvas ½" from the stitching all the way around.

Cut mat board (available in art supply stores) into six pieces: four for the sides, one for the top, and one for the bottom. They should be *exactly* the size of the stitching except for the rows of Half Cross Stitches that will be the corners. Use a mat knife and metal-edged ruler to cut the mat board.

Glue each piece of mat board to the wrong side of the stitching (Figure 16-7a). (Fabric glue does nicely.) Pull the edges of canvas around to the back side of the mat board. Miter the corners as shown in the photo series on framing (page 251). Glue all canvas edges in place. Clip pinch-type clothespins around the edges to hold the canvas down while the glue dries. Move them often, or they will stick to the needlepoint.

For the bottom, cut a piece of felt ½" larger on all sides than the bottom mat-board piece. Wrap the felt around the

FIG. 16-7a–e
Finishing Jody's Needlepoint Box.

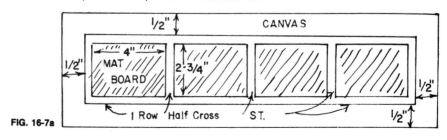

FIG. 16-7a

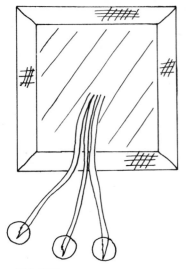

FIG. 16-7b

bottom piece of mat board just as you did the canvas above. Hold with the clothespins till it dries.

The lining fabric should be lightweight and pretty. Crepe-backed satin in your main color makes an elegant lining. You'll need about a quarter of a yard. You'll also need thread to match.

The lining is padded with bonded Dacron quilt batting. Cut six pieces of batting the same sizes as you have cut the mat board—four the same size for the sides and two the same size for the top and bottom. The batting should be about ½" thick.

Press the lining fabric to remove wrinkles. Then cut three pieces of fabric ½" larger on all sides than the stitched pieces of canvas and ½" larger on all sides than the bottom. The side sections will be one long piece of fabric—even though the mat board and quilt batting are in separate pieces.

Tie bells or beads onto three or five pieces of yarn. Glue onto the mat-board side of the top of the box (Figure 16-7b).

Glue the puffs of quilt batting to the backs of each section of mat board. See Figure 16-7c for a cross-section view.

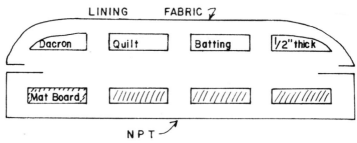

LINING   FABRIC

Dacron | Quilt | Batting | ½" thick

Mat Board | ///////// | /// ///// | ///// /////

N P T

FIG. 16-7c

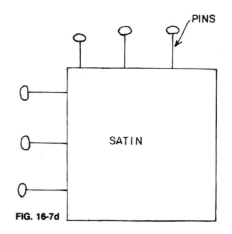

PINS

SATIN

FIG. 16-7d

Turn under the raw edges of the lining fabric ¼". Pin it into the edges of the mat board (Figure 16-7d). Stitch in place with sewing thread.

The Blind Stitch (page 255) makes your stitches invisible. Or you may Overcast the edges. Line the top and bottom pieces, too.

After you've stitched the long piece of lining in place, gently bend this piece of lined, padded needlepoint at each row of Tent Stitches. The lining will automatically tuck in between the pads of quilt batting. Whipstitch the open corner together with the main color yarn. Use one ply (Figure 16-7e).

Turn the side pieces so that the bottom is up. Put the bottom in place, with the lining to the inside. Sew it in place with sewing thread. Catch both the felt and the needlepoint. Insert the needle into the felt and then the needlepoint. Take another stitch in the needlepoint and then through to the felt. Take another stitch in the felt and then in the needlepoint. Continue, easing in the felt if necessary.

Using one ply of yarn, attach the top with an Overcast Stitch. But stitch only the side opposite the one where your bells or beads are attached. Make your stitches loose, so that the lid will lie flat. These stitches will serve as a hinge.

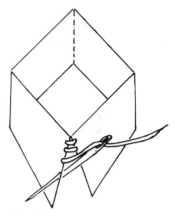

FIG. 16-7e

Christmas wreath

Cut a plywood board according to the measurements in Figure 16-8a. Buy a string of miniature Christmas lights with red bulbs. (These will be your holly berries.) Drill holes big enough for three of the bulbs to go through (one at a time). Space the holes according to the length of the wire between bulbs.

Staple the outer edges of the canvas to the outer edges of the circular board. Ease the canvas in, and match up the holes as you go.

Insert one light bulb through a hole in the wood and then through the corresponding hole on the needlepoint. Bring two more through the same holes—one at a time. Leave some slack in the wire so the wreath can be stuffed. You now have a cluster of three red holly berries.

Following the dotted line in Figure 16-8a, continue around the board, putting three lights in each hole as just described. Anchor the wires with special staples for electric wire on the back side of the board (check with the hardware store).

Finishing

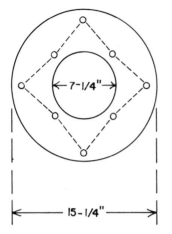

FIG. 16-8a *Cutting plywood board for wreath.*

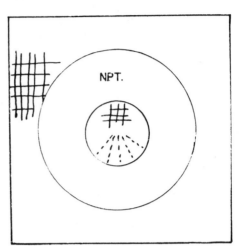

FIG. 16-8b *Cutting needlepoint wreath.*

Slash the blank needlepoint canvas in the middle, almost to the stitching (Figure 16-8b). Cut all the way around. Stuff the wreath with polyester fiber filling from the center hole. Be careful not to disturb the wires.

Pull the pieces of canvas in the center hole to the back, and staple. If the canvas is not turning back neatly, slash it more often—*not* deeper.

Cover the back with felt. Attach a sawtooth hanger. Glue green velvet ribbon on the inside and outside edges of the wreath. Attach a large red velvet bow.

Retail mail order sources

PRODUCT	SOURCE
Bird Cage	Doyle Raymer P.O. Box 9 Van Buren, Missouri 63965
Bulletin Board	Just-So Frame Co. 2502 Heritage Trail Enid, Oklahoma 73701
Headlights	Sheru Enterprises, Inc. 49 West 38th Street New York, New York 10018
Ribbon	Patricia Mabry Enterprises, Inc. P.O. Box 523 Fairfield, Alabama 35064

PRODUCT	SOURCE
Silver Kid	Elsa T. Cose Hadlar Drive, R.D. 3 Lebanon, New Jersey 08833
Walnut Items (Table, Mirror, Box, City Park Base)	Murray's Joinery Works 1017 John Adams Drive Biloxi, Mississippi 39531

Index

General index

Acrylic paints, 14, 32, 33
Airplane, 74–77
Apple, 127–28
Apple tree mirror, 51–52
Appliqué, 107–28
  apple, 127–28
  car, 118–21
  landscape table top, 107–17
  mother and child, 121–26

Ballet slippers, 40–42
Basket of flowers, 67–70
Beginning yarns, 21
Bell pull, 56–60
Bird necklace, 73
Black cat, 133–37
Black-eyed susan purse, 49–51
Blocking, 239–46
  board, 239–40
  correcting distortion, 29, 244–46
  fastening the canvas, 243
  fluffing raised stitches, 244
  grid pattern, 240
  removing stains, 244

reviving limp pieces, 244
steps in, 241–43
Blooming End, 19
Breakaway (waste) canvas, 9
Bulletin board, 88–90

Canvas, 3–9
  breakaway (waste), 9
  cleaning, 30–31
  fastening to blocking board, 243
  interlock Mono, 5, 6, 18
  mesh count, 6–7
  needle size and, 9
  Penelope, 4
  plastic, 8
  preparation of, 18
  regular Mono, 4–5, 6
  stitch size, 8
Car, 118–21
Christmas mobile, 71–72
Christmas wreath:
  detached canvas, 84–88
  finishing, 259–60
  raised stitch, 48–49

City park, 137–47
Cleaning needlepoint, 30–31
Compensating stitches, 28
Continuous motion, 24–25
Cube, 43–45

Designs:
  enlarging or reducing, 31–32
  transferring, 32–33
Detached canvas, 84–106
  bulletin board, 88–90
  Christmas wreath, 84–88
  house, 101–6
  intertwined rainbows, 91–101
Direction of stitching, 28
Direction of work, 26
Distortion, correcting, 29, 244–46

Embroidery floss, 12, 46
Embroidery hoop, 16
Ending yarns, 21–23
Enlarging designs, 31–32

Farm, 63–66

Finishing, 239–60
  blocking, 239–46
    board, 239–40
    correcting distortion, 29,
      244–46
    fastening the canvas, 245
    fluffing raised stitches, 244
    grid pattern, 240
    removing stains, 244
    reviving limp pieces, 244
    steps in, 241–43
  Christmas wreath, 259–60
  framing, 14–15, 247–53
  Jody's needlepoint box, 257–59
  pillows, 253–57
    construction, 254–55
    inserts, 253–54
    linings, 257
    twisted cord, 255–57
Four-seasons bell pull, 56–60
Framing, 14–15, 247–53

Golf trophy, 77–83
Grid method, 32
Grid pattern, 240

House, 101–6
  framing, 253

Interlock Mono canvas, 5, 6, 18
Intertwined rainbows, 91–101
  framing, 253

Jody's needlepoint box, 53–56
  finishing, 257–59

Label, yarn, 17
Landscape table top, 107–17
Left-handed needlepoint, 31
Linings, pillow, 257
Lithographer, 31

Mail order sources, 261–62
Masking tape, 14
Mending, 29–30
Mesh count, 6–7
Metallic yarn, 12, 13
Mirror, 51–52
Mixed media, 129–52
  black cat, 133–37
  city park, 137–47
  needlepoint shop, 129–32
  northwest autumn, 147–51
  waste knot, want knot, 151–52
Mobile, 71–72

Mono canvas:
  interlock, 5, 6, 18
  regular, 4–5, 6
Mother and child, 121–26

Nap, 19
Needlepoint box, 53–56
  finishing, 257–59
Needlepoint shop, 129–32
Needles, 9–11, 20–21
Needle threader, 10
Northwest autumn, 147–51
  framing, 253
Novelty yarns, 12–13, 18

Optical illusion with color and line,
  39–47
  ballet slippers, 40–42
  cube, 43–45
  stacked boxes, 39–40
  triangle, 46–47
Over-under weaving method, 21–23

Pearl cotton, 12, 13
Penelope canvas, 4
Persian yarn, 12, 18–20
Pillows, finishing, 253–57
  construction, 254–55
  inserts, 253–54
  linings, 257
  twisted cord, 255–57
Plastic canvas, 8
Procedures, basic, 16–35
  beginning and ending yarns,
    21–23
  canvas preparation, 18
  cleaning needlepoint, 30–31
  compensating stitches, 28
  continuous motion, 24–25
  correcting distortion, 29, 244–46
  direction of stitching, 28
  direction of work, 26
  enlarging or reducing designs,
    31–32
  handling yarn, 18–19
  keeping yarn, 16–17
  left-handed needlepoint, 31
  mixing diagonal and vertical
    stitches, 28
  ripping and mending, 29–30
  rolling yarn, 23–24
  stab method, 25
  stitching with yarn, 19–29
  stripping yarn, 19–21
  tension, 26

thickening and thinning yarn,
  26–28
transferring designs, 32–33
Projects (see Three-dimensional
  needlepoint)
Purse, 49–51

Raised stitches, 48–66
  apple tree mirror, 51–52
  black-eyed susan purse, 49–51
  Christmas wreath ornament,
    48–49
  farm, 63–66
  fluffing, 244
  four seasons bell pull, 56–60
  Jody's needlepoint box, 53–56
  scissors case, 61–62
Rayon floss, 12, 13
Reducing designs, 31–32
Regular Mono canvas, 4–5, 6
Retail mail order sources, 261–62
Ribbon, 12, 13
Ripping, 29–30
Rolling yarn, 23–24
Round needlepoint, 67–83
  airplane, 74–77
  basket of flowers, 67–70
  bird necklace, 73
  Christmas mobile, 71–72
  golf trophy, 77–83
Ruler, 14

Scissors, 14
Scissors case, 61–62
Sources, mail order, 261–62
Stab method, 25
Stacked boxes, 39–40
Stains, removal of, 244
Staple gun, 243
Stitch tension, 26
Stripping yarn, 19–21
Supplies, 3–15
  acrylic paints, 14, 32, 33
  canvas, 3–9
    breakaway (waste), 9
    cleaning, 30–31
    fastening to blocking board,
      243
    interlock Mono, 5, 6, 18
    mesh count, 6–7
    needle size and, 9
    Penelope, 4
    plastic, 8
    preparation of, 18
    regular Mono, 4–5, 6
    stitch size, 8

Supplies (cont'd.)
frame, 14–15, 247–53
masking tape, 14
needles, 9–11, 20–21
ruler, 14
scissors, 14
staple gun, 243
tweezers, 14
waterproof marker, 14, 32, 240, 241, 248–49
yarn, 11–13
amount needed, 13
beginning and ending, 21–23
cleaning, 30–31
handling, 18–19
keeping, 16–17
novelty, 12–13, 18
Persian, 12, 18–20
rolling, 23–24
stitching with, 19–29
stripping, 19–21
tapestry, 12, 18–19
thickening and thinning, 26–28
threading on needle, 9–11

Table top, 107–17
Tapestry yarns, 12, 18–19
Tension, 26
Thickening and thinning yarn, 26–28
Three-dimensional needlepoint:
appliqué, 107–28
apple, 127–28

car, 118–21
landscape table top, 107–17
mother and child, 121–26
detached canvas, 84–106
bulletin board, 88–90
Christmas wreath, 84–88
house, 101–6
intertwined rainbows, 91–101
mixed media, 129–52
black cat, 133–37
city park, 137–47
needlepoint shop, 129–32
northwest autumn, 147–51
waste knot, want knot, 151–52
optical illusion with color and line, 39–47
ballet slippers, 40–42
cube, 43–45
stacked boxes, 39–40
triangle, 46–47
raised stitches, 48–66
apple tree mirror, 51–52
black-eyed susan purse, 49–51
Christmas wreath ornament, 48–49
farm, 63–66
four seasons bell pull, 56–60
Jody's needlepoint box, 53–56
scissors case, 61–62
round, 67–83
airplane, 74–77
basket of flowers, 67–70
bird necklace, 73

Christmas mobile, 71–72
golf trophy, 77–83
Transferring designs, 32–33
Triangle, 46–47
Tweezers, 14
Twisted cord, 255–57
Two-step edge-finishing method, 57

Velvet or velour yarn, 12

Waste canvas, 9
Waste knot, 21
Waste knot, want knot, 151–52
Watermarks, 243
Waterproof marker, 14, 32, 240, 241, 248–49

Yarn, 11–13
amount needed, 13
beginning and ending, 21–23
cleaning, 30–31
handling, 18–19
keeping, 16–17
novelty, 12–13, 18
Persian, 12, 18–20
rolling, 23–24
stitching with, 19–29
stripping, 19–21
tapestry, 12, 18–19
thickening and thinning, 26–28
threading on needle, 9–11

Stitch Index

Backstitch, 27, 28, 43, 46, 57, 74, 137
Bargello, 6, 18, 40, 41, 107, 108, 109, 129, 130, 162–63
Bargello framework pattern, 164
Bargello line pattern, 163
Basketweave, 4–5, 39, 40, 51, 61, 73, 74, 77, 84, 88, 91, 101, 103, 121, 129, 147, 167–69, 172
Binding Stitch, 48, 57, 61, 62, 71, 72, 74, 75, 77, 81, 82, 88, 103, 104, 198–99, 243
Blind Stitch, 126, 254, 259

Box stitches, 179–91
Brick, 121, 158
Bullion Knots, 61, 63, 121, 126, 227
Buttonhole, 67, 68, 84, 87, 88, 108, 219
Buttonhole in Half-Circle, 137, 220
Byzantine, 67, 127
Byzantine #1, 176
Byzantine #3, 63, 177

Cashmere, 118, 137, 183
Chain, 108, 109, 118, 221
Close Herringbone, 57, 63, 215

Continental, 39, 40, 63, 74, 77, 84, 101, 118, 121, 129, 133, 137, 168, 169–70, 172
Couching, 40, 41, 57, 63, 121, 208
Cross Stitch, 194
Cross stitches, 6, 56, 192–204
Cut Turkey Work, 56, 61, 63, 77, 101, 133, 137, 230

Decorative stitches, 217–36
Diagonal Cashmere, 63, 77, 186
Diagonal Mosaic, 88, 182
Diagonal stitches, 28, 165–78

Diamond Ray, 57, *212*
Double Brick, 40, *159*
Double Leviathan, 53, *202*
Double Star, *211*
Double Stitch, 74, *196*
Double Straight Cross, 61, *201*

Elongated Cashmere, 137, *185*
Eye stitches, 208–11

Fly, *207*
F-106, *161*
Framed Cashmere, 101, *184*
Framed Scotch, 101, *190*
Framed Star, *210*
Frame Stitch, 27
French Knots, 27, 48, 49, 56, 61, 63, 137, 147, *225*
French Knots on Stalks, 57, 61, 63, *226*

Giant Brick, 43, *159*
Giant Cashmere, 137
Giant Scotch, 49, 137, *188*
Gross Point, 8

Half Cross, 53, *171*
Horizontal Brick, 101, *160*
Hungarian, 88, 118, *161*

Interlocking Gobelin, 63, 74, 107, *174*

Knotted Stitch, 63, *207*

Lazy Daisy, *231*
Lazy Kalem, 118, *174*
Leaf #1, 71, 101, *214*
Leaf stitches, 105, 212–16
Long Stitch, 88, 89
Looped Turkey Work, 49, 51, 61, 63, 104, 105, 108, 133, 137, *229*

Mosaic, 26, 48, 57, 67, 77, 137, *181*

Needleweaving, 49, 61, 63, 88, 133, *231*

Oriental, 118, *178*
Overcast Stitch, 72, 77, 103, 104, 105, 145, 146, 259

Petit Point, 8, 63, *172*
Plaited Gobelin, *200*
Plaited Herringbone, 63

Quickpoint, 8

Raised Band, 48, 49, 51, 127
Raised Buttonhole, 48, 49, 51, 127, 147, *234*
Raised Buttonhole on Raised Band, 63, *235*
Raised Close Herringbone, 51, 63, *216*
Raised Cup Stitch, 63, *232–33*
Raised Rope, 57, 61, 63, *233*
Ray, 61, 63, *213*
Reversed Mosaic, 57, *182*
Reversed Scotch, 84, 127, 133, *191*

Rice, *195*
Ridged Spider Web, 61, 63, *224*
Roumanian Leaf, 127, *215*

Scotch, 26, 67, 137, *187*
Shingle, 101, *160*
Shisha, 118, 133, *235–36*
Slanted Cross, *197*
Slanted Gobelin, 71, 72
Slanted Gobelin 2 x 2, 53, *173*
Slashed Cross, *197*
Smooth Spider Web, 57, 61, 74, *223*
Smyrna Cross, 53, *204*
Spider Webs, 51, *221–22*
Split Gobelin, 101, *158*
Split Slanted Gobelin, *173*
Starfish, 61, 63, *228*
Stem, *175*
Straight Gobelin, 74, *157*
Straight stitches, 6, 46, 63, 74, 101, 133, 137, 147, 155–64

Tent stitches, 165–71, 259
Thorn, 63, *228*
Tied Scotch, *189*
Tied stitches, 205–8
Tied Windmill, 71, 72, *203*
Tramé, 27
2 x 2 Cross, 63, *195*

Upright Cross, 118, 121, 145, *196*

Waffle Stitch, 23
Wound Cross, 56, 61, 63, *224*
Woven Spider Web, 56, 61, 221, *223*